W9-BCY-494

# Immigration Bans

# Other Books of Related Interest

## Opposing Viewpoints Series

American Values
Civil Liberties
Human Rights
Illegal Immigration

## At Issue Series

Immigration Reform
Mexico's Drug War
Should the US Close Its Borders?
What Rights Should Illegal Immigrants Have?

## Current Controversies Series

Homeland Security
Illegal Immigration
Islamophobia
Jobs in America

"Congress shall make
no law … abridging
the freedom of speech,
or of the press."

*First Amendment to the US Constitution*

The basic foundation of our democracy is the First Amendment guarantee of freedom of expression. The Opposing Viewpoints series is dedicated to the concept of this basic freedom and the idea that it is more important to practice it than to enshrine it.

# Immigration Bans

**Elizabeth Schmermund, Book Editor**

Published in 2018 by Greenhaven Publishing, LLC
353 3rd Avenue, Suite 255, New York, NY 10010

Articles in Greenhaven Publishing anthologies are often edited for length to meet page
requirements. In addition, original titles of these works are changed to clearly present
the main thesis and to explicitly indicate the author's opinion. Every effort is made to
ensure that Greenhaven Publishing accurately reflects the original intent of the authors.
Every effort has been made to trace the owners of the copyrighted material.

Cover image: Chess Ocampo/Shutterstock.com

**Library of Congress Cataloging-in-Publication Data**

Names: Schmermund, Elizabeth, editor.
Title: Immigration bans / edited by Elizabeth Schmermund.
Description: First edition. | New York, NY : Greenhaven Publishing, 2018. | Series:
Opposing Viewpoints | Includes bibliographical references and index. | Audience:
Grade 9 to 12.
Identifiers: LCCN 2017004976| ISBN 9781534500594 (library bound) | ISBN
9781534500570 (pbk.)
Subjects: LCSH: Immigrants--Government policy--United States--Juvenile
literature. | United States--Emigration and immigration--Government
policy--Juvenile literature.
Classification: LCC JV6483 .I5537 2018 | DDC 325.73--dc23
LC record available at https://lccn.loc.gov/2017004976

Manufactured in the United States of America

Website: http://greenhavenpublishing.com

# Contents

## Chapter 3: How Much Does the US Economy Rely on Immigrant Labor?

## Chapter 4: Do Increased Border Control and Deportations Actually Work?

# The Importance of Opposing Viewpoints

Perhaps every generation experiences a period in time in which the populace seems especially polarized, starkly divided on the important issues of the day and gravitating toward the far ends of the political spectrum and away from a consensus-facilitating middle ground. The world that today's students are growing up in and that they will soon enter into as active and engaged citizens is deeply fragmented in just this way. Issues relating to terrorism, immigration, women's rights, minority rights, race relations, health care, taxation, wealth and poverty, the environment, policing, military intervention, the proper role of government—in some ways, perennial issues that are freshly and uniquely urgent and vital with each new generation—are currently roiling the world.

If we are to foster a knowledgeable, responsible, active, and engaged citizenry among today's youth, we must provide them with the intellectual, interpretive, and critical-thinking tools and experience necessary to make sense of the world around them and of the all-important debates and arguments that inform it. After all, the outcome of these debates will in large measure determine the future course, prospects, and outcomes of the world and its peoples, particularly its youth. If they are to become successful members of society and productive and informed citizens, students need to learn how to evaluate the strengths and weaknesses of someone else's arguments, how to sift fact from opinion and fallacy, and how to test the relative merits and validity of their own opinions against the known facts and the best possible available information. The landmark series Opposing Viewpoints has been providing students with just such critical-thinking skills and exposure to the debates surrounding society's most urgent contemporary issues for many years, and it continues to serve this essential role with undiminished commitment, care, and rigor.

The key to the series's success in achieving its goal of sharpening students' critical-thinking and analytic skills resides in its title—

Opposing Viewpoints. In every intriguing, compelling, and engaging volume of this series, readers are presented with the widest possible spectrum of distinct viewpoints, expert opinions, and informed argumentation and commentary, supplied by some of today's leading academics, thinkers, analysts, politicians, policy makers, economists, activists, change agents, and advocates. Every opinion and argument anthologized here is presented objectively and accorded respect. There is no editorializing in any introductory text or in the arrangement and order of the pieces. No piece is included as a "straw man," an easy ideological target for cheap point-scoring. As wide and inclusive a range of viewpoints as possible is offered, with no privileging of one particular political ideology or cultural perspective over another. It is left to each individual reader to evaluate the relative merits of each argument— as he or she sees it, and with the use of ever-growing critical-thinking skills—and grapple with his or her own assumptions, beliefs, and perspectives to determine how convincing or successful any given argument is and how the reader's own stance on the issue may be modified or altered in response to it.

This process is facilitated and supported by volume, chapter, and selection introductions that provide readers with the essential context they need to begin engaging with the spotlighted issues, with the debates surrounding them, and with their own perhaps shifting or nascent opinions on them. In addition, guided reading and discussion questions encourage readers to determine the authors' point of view and purpose, interrogate and analyze the various arguments and their rhetoric and structure, evaluate the arguments' strengths and weaknesses, test their claims against available facts and evidence, judge the validity of the reasoning, and bring into clearer, sharper focus the reader's own beliefs and conclusions and how they may differ from or align with those in the collection or those of their classmates.

Research has shown that reading comprehension skills improve dramatically when students are provided with compelling, intriguing, and relevant "discussable" texts. The subject matter of these collections could not be more compelling, intriguing, or urgently relevant to today's students and the world they are poised to inherit. The anthologized articles and the reading and discussion questions that are included with them also provide the basis for stimulating, lively, and passionate classroom debates. Students who are compelled to anticipate objections to their own argument and identify the flaws in those of an opponent read more carefully, think more critically, and steep themselves in relevant context, facts, and information more thoroughly. In short, using discussable text of the kind provided by every single volume in the Opposing Viewpoints series encourages close reading, facilitates reading comprehension, fosters research, strengthens critical thinking, and greatly enlivens and energizes classroom discussion and participation. The entire learning process is deepened, extended, and strengthened.

For all of these reasons, Opposing Viewpoints continues to be exactly the right resource at exactly the right time—when we most need to provide readers with the critical-thinking tools and skills that will not only serve them well in school but also in their careers and their daily lives as decision-making family members, community members, and citizens. This series encourages respectful engagement with and analysis of opposing viewpoints and fosters a resulting increase in the strength and rigor of one's own opinions and stances. As such, it helps make readers "future ready," and that readiness will pay rich dividends for the readers themselves, for the citizenry, for our society, and for the world at large.

# Introduction

Immigration can be a contentious issue—and can even dictate a political party's platform—not only in the United States but in countries around the world. This is because of how people view their national identity—their role in their government and their government's place in their lives. Oftentimes, immigrants disrupt people's views of themselves and their countries. It can be difficult—and has proved to be difficult historically—not to blame immigrants for economic woes. Unfortunately, immigrants are often blamed for job losses, for safety concerns, or for petty crimes even when statistics do not provide any evidence for this.

Bans on immigration have long been in effect in the United States in order to deal with these fears and perceptions. Oftentimes, people believe that a country will descend into chaos without a quota system for letting in immigrants. This is particularly true for relatively economically stable and, indeed, prosperous countries like the United States, in which immigrants have long been seen as a "problem" that needs to be stopped (or, rather, staunched) for continued political power and economic success. As the saying goes, America is great because of its people. But who constitutes its people?

This is a question that is not so easy to answer. As some people are fond of saying, the United States is an immigrant nation largely developed by immigrants who not only defined what it meant to be American but also defined the trajectory of the nation itself. Immigration bans were in place even back during this formative moment in the nation's history, in the nineteenth century, when immigration to the United States exploded, particularly from Europe. During this time, waves of Italians, Irish, and Germans entered the country through Ellis Island in New York Harbor. In the western United States, Chinese laborers entered California. They came looking for economic opportunities and increased freedoms and, at least initially, sometimes found prejudice and hardship. The Chinese Exclusion Act, passed in 1882, was one of the first of these new immigration bans, which barred Chinese laborers from entering the country and legalized the deportation of any unauthorized Chinese immigrants. The 1891 Immigration Act continued to permit deportation of any unauthorized immigrants, not just the Chinese, and established the federal Bureau of Immigration. A further immigration act in 1917 banned immigration from all Asian countries except for the Philippines, which was a US colony at the time. By the 1920s, border control had been implemented along with a national quota system based on the nationality of immigrants. The 1920s began the precedent for how the United States would deal with this newly perceived "problem" of immigration. Only in the 1960s would new changes be made to the US immigration system, keeping a quota system while adding preferences for skilled workers and priorities for family reunification.

Today, it seems like these questions of who is let into the United States and how that's decided are as contentious as ever before. During economic booms in the 1990s, immigration into the United States soared, while the economic crisis in 2008 led to dwindling numbers of immigrants entering into the country. Yet large-scale crises around the globe, particularly in the Middle East and North Africa (Syria, Iraq, Afghanistan, and Libya) and in Africa (Sudan and Somalia), have created a global refugee crisis in recent years with some 65 million refugees in the world today. These refugees, forced from their home by famine, terrorism, and war, have no other choice but to attempt a treacherous trek from their homes to new and unfamiliar countries, where most are settled in refugee camps that lack basic comforts. Some countries, like Germany, have taken a leading role in accepting and resettling refugees while others, like the United States, have been much more reticent. Notably, many US politicians have declared that there should be an outright ban on all Syrian refugees in the United

States for security purposes, including on orphaned children as young as five. Refugee and immigrant activists have spoken out against these proposed bans as being unethical and irresponsible.

With this highly politicized climate in which new questions about immigration are playing out, it is easy to listen to only one side of the story or to accept everything we hear as true. However, it is more important than ever before to take in a wide variety of viewpoints surrounding immigration, to consider where these opinions might be coming from and what motives they might have, and then draw our own conclusions. In *Opposing Viewpoints: Immigration Bans,* authors tackle the important questions from many perspectives in chapters titled "How Have Immigration Bans Had Different Effects on Ethnic, Religious, Racial, or Socioeconomic Groups?," "How Can We Reconcile Humanitarian and Security Concerns for Refugees and Immigrants?," "How Much Does the US Economy Rely on Immigrant Labor?," and "Do Increased Border Control and Deportations Actually Work?" The refugee crisis and immigration will continue to be pressing issues in coming years, and we must all give our attention to them now in order to make informed, rational, and ethical decisions in the future.

CHAPTER 1

# How Have Immigration Bans Had Different Effects on Ethnic, Religious, Racial, or Socioeconomic Groups?

# Chapter Preface

I mmigration bans have always affected different groups of people in different ways. While borders were historically open for many people (mostly European immigrants) from the eighteenth century until the late nineteenth century, the Chinese Exclusion Act of 1882 set a precedent by prohibiting the immigration of all workers from a particular country. This law was passed in the wake of anti-Chinese sentiment, which was drummed up by politicians during a period of economic hardship following the Civil War. In the early twentieth century, a "gentleman's agreement" was arrived at between Japan and the United States, which severely limited the amount of Japanese immigrants into the country.

The period following World War I, which saw decreased amounts of immigration into the United States, ushered in an age of national quotas. Beginning in 1924, several laws were passed that limited immigration based on country of origin, with the express intent being to prevent immigration from changing the ethnic distribution of the US population. During this time, western Europeans were generally allowed into the country, while Africans, southern Europeans, and Asians were more restricted. However, there were not yet bans on Latin Americans immigrating into the country. This so-called "National Origins Formula" was repealed in 1965. It was replaced by two quotas, one for immigrants from the Western Hemisphere, set at 120,000 immigrants per year, and one for immigrants from the Eastern Hemisphere, set at 170,000 immigrants per year. These quotas were eventually combined and dictated on a country-by-country basis.

The 1990s ushered in a period of time during which skilled immigrants were given precedence over unskilled workers. This continues to be championed by many advocates of reform to the current immigration system. However, it is undeniable that skilled immigrants come from higher social classes, as they have the money and the flexibility to pay for advanced educations. Critics of this system state that it unduly benefits richer populations while further restricting the poor from entry into the United States, thus encouraging them to take illegal routes in.

The history of the immigration system in the United States shows that national origin, ethnicity, and social class have been used by the government to deem who will be granted entry into the country and who must be kept out. Many researchers in the field state that this continues today, particularly in the treatment of wealthier citizens from western Europe compared to poorer residents of the global south. While some commentators suggest that this is a purely practical way of restricting immigration to those who will best contribute to the economy, others state that this is an essentially racist and classist immigration system that gives precedence to capital over people in need. In this chapter, we will explore this issue from all sides of the debate.

> "*Like many other settler societies,
> the United States, before it achieved
> independence and afterward, relied
> on the flow of newcomers from
> abroad to people its relatively open
> and unsettled lands.*"

# The United States Has Historically Depended on Immigrant Labor

*Hasia Diner*

*In the following viewpoint, Hasia Diner examines five distinct historical periods of immigration and how they compare with our contemporary moment. Diner begins with a description of the United States as a "settler nation" that needed immigrant labor in order to develop its economy and continued to need this labor until it was largely curtailed during modern nativist movements in the twentieth century. While stereotypes about immigrants continue to abound today, Diner states, immigrants who arrive in the United States largely search to assimilate to American culture and ways of living. Diner is a professor of American Jewish history at New York University.*

"Immigration in U.S. History," by Hasia Diner, 2009. Reprinted by permission.

As you read, consider the following questions:

1. What historical link does immigration share with imperialism?
2. What are the five distinct historical periods of immigration that the author names?
3. What is nativism? When does the author claim nativism became a major movement in the United States and why?

Millions of women and men from around the world have decided to immigrate to the United States. That fact constitutes one of the central elements in the country's overall development, involving a process fundamental to its pre-national origins, its emergence as a new and independent nation, and its subsequent rise from being an Atlantic outpost to a world power, particularly in terms of its economic growth. Immigration has made the United States of America.

Like many other settler societies, the United States, before it achieved independence and afterward, relied on the flow of newcomers from abroad to people its relatively open and unsettled lands. It shared this historical reality with Canada, South Africa, Australia, New Zealand, and Argentina, among other nations.

In all of these cases the imperial powers that claimed these places had access to two of the three elements essential to fulfilling their goal of extracting natural resources from the colony. They had land and capital but lacked people to do the farming, lumbering, mining, hunting, and the like. Colonial administrators tried to use native labor, with greater or lesser success, and they abetted the escalation of the African slave trade, bringing millions of migrants, against their will, to these New World outposts.

Immigration, however, played a key role not only in making America's development possible but also in shaping the basic nature of the society. Its history falls into five distinct time periods, each of which involved varying rates of migration from distinctly different places in the world. Each reflected, and also shaped, much about the basic nature of American society and economy.

## Settlers of the New World

The first, and longest, era stretched from the 17th century through the early 19th century. Immigrants came from a range of places, including the German-speaking area of the Palatinate, France (Protestant Huguenots), and the Netherlands. Other immigrants were Jews, also from the Netherlands and from Poland, but most immigrants of this era tended to hail from the British Isles, with English, Scottish, Welsh, and Ulster Irish gravitating toward different colonies (later states) and regions.

These immigrants, usually referred to as settlers, opted in the main for farming, with the promise of cheap land a major draw for relatively impoverished northern and western Europeans who found themselves unable to take advantage of the modernization of their home economies. One group of immigrants deserves some special attention because their experience sheds much light on the forces impelling migration. In this era, considerable numbers of women and men came as indentured servants. They entered into contracts with employers who specified the time and conditions of labor in exchange for passage to the New World. While they endured harsh conditions during their time of service, as a result of their labors, they acquired ownership of small pieces of land that they could then work as independent yeoman farmers.

## Mass migration

The numbers who came during this era were relatively small. That changed, however, by the 1820s. This period ushered in the first era of mass migration. From that decade through the 1880s, about 15 million immigrants made their way to the United States, many choosing agriculture in the Midwest and Northeast, while others flocked to cities like New York, Philadelphia, Boston, and Baltimore.

Factors in both Europe and the United States shaped this transition. The end of the Napoleonic Wars in Europe liberated young men from military service back home at the same time that industrialization and agricultural consolidation in England, Scandinavia, and much of central Europe transformed local economies and created a class of young people who could not earn a living in the new order. Demand for immigrant labor shot up with two major developments: the settlement of the American Midwest after the inauguration of the Erie Canal in 1825 and the related rise of the port of New York, and the first stirrings of industrial development in the United States, particularly in textile production, centered in New England.

Immigrants tended to cluster by group in particular neighborhoods, cities, and regions. The American Midwest, as it emerged in the middle of the 19th century as one of the world's most fertile agricultural regions, became home to tight-knit, relatively homogeneous communities of immigrants from Sweden, Norway, Denmark, Bohemia, and various regions of what in 1871 would become Germany.

This era saw the first large-scale arrival of Catholic immigrants to the largely Protestant United States, and these primarily Irish women and men inspired the nation's first serious bout of nativism, which combined an antipathy to immigrants in general with a fear of Catholicism and an aversion to the Irish. Particularly in the decades just before the U.S. Civil War (1861-1865), this nativism spawned a powerful political movement and even a political party, the Know Nothings, which made anti-immigration and anti-Catholicism central to its political agenda. This period also witnessed the arrival of small numbers of Chinese men to the American West. Native-born Americans reacted intensely and negatively to their arrival, leading to the passage of the only piece of U.S. immigration legislation that specifically named a group as the focus of restrictive policy, the Chinese Exclusion Act of 1882.

## A wave becomes a flood

Gradually over the course of the decades after the Civil War, as the sources of immigration shifted so too did the technology of ocean travel. Whereas previous immigrants had made their way to the United States via sail power, innovations in steam transportation made it possible for larger ships to bring larger loads of immigrants to the United States. The immigrants of this era tended to come from southern and eastern Europe, regions undergoing at the end of the 19th and beginning of the 20th centuries the same economic transitions that western and northern Europe had earlier experienced.

As among the immigrants of the earlier period, young people predominated among the newcomers. This wave of migration, which constituted the third episode in the history of U.S. immigration, could better be referred to as a flood of immigrants, as nearly 25 million Europeans made the voyage. Italians, Greeks, Hungarians, Poles, and others speaking Slavic languages constituted the bulk of this migration. Included among them were 2.5 to 3 million Jews.

Each group evinced a distinctive migration pattern in terms of the gender balance within the migratory pool, the permanence of their migration, their literacy rates, the balance between adults and children, and the like. But they shared one overarching characteristic: They flocked to urban destinations and made up the bulk of the U.S. industrial labor pool, making possible the emergence of such industries as steel, coal, automobile, textile, and garment production, and enabling the United States to leap into the front ranks of the world's economic giants.

Their urban destinations, their numbers, and perhaps a fairly basic human antipathy towards foreigners led to the emergence of a second wave of organized xenophobia. By the 1890s, many Americans, particularly from the ranks of the well-off, white, native-born, considered immigration to pose a serious danger to the nation's health and security. In 1893 a group of them formed the Immigration Restriction League, and it, along with other similarly inclined organizations, began to press Congress for severe curtailment of foreign immigration.

## Legislating immigration

Restriction proceeded piecemeal over the course of the late 19th and early 20th centuries, but immediately after the end of World War I (1914-1918) and into the early 1920s, Congress did change the nation's basic policy about immigration. The National Origins Act in 1921 (and its final form in 1924) not only restricted the number of immigrants who might enter the United States but also assigned slots according to quotas based on national origins. A complicated piece of legislation, it essentially gave preference to immigrants from northern and western Europe, severely limited the numbers from eastern and southern Europe, and declared all potential immigrants from Asia to be unworthy of entry into the United States.

The legislation excluded the Western Hemisphere from the quota system, and the 1920s ushered in the penultimate era in U.S. immigration history. Immigrants could and did move quite freely from Mexico, the Caribbean (including Jamaica, Barbados, and Haiti), and other parts of Central and South America. This era, which reflected the application of the 1924 legislation, lasted until 1965. During those 40 years, the United States began to admit, case by case, limited numbers of refugees. Jewish refugees from Nazi Germany before World War II, Jewish Holocaust survivors after the war, non-Jewish displaced persons fleeing Communist rule in eastern Europe, Hungarians seeking refuge after their failed uprising in 1956, and Cubans after the 1960 revolution managed to find haven in the United States because their plight moved the conscience of Americans, but the basic immigration law remained in place.

## The Hart-Celler Act

This all changed with passage of the Hart-Celler Act in 1965, a by-product of the civil rights revolution and a jewel in the crown of President Lyndon Johnson's Great Society programs. The measure had not been intended to stimulate immigration from Asia, the Middle East, Africa, and elsewhere in the developing world. Rather, by doing away with the racially based quota system, its authors had expected that immigrants would come from the "traditional" sending societies such as Italy, Greece, and Poland, places that labored under very small quotas in the 1924 law. The law replaced the quotas with preference categories based on family relationships and job skills, giving particular preference to potential immigrants with relatives in the United States and with occupations deemed critical by the U.S. Department of Labor. But after 1970, following an initial influx from those European countries, immigrants began to hail from places like Korea, China, India, the Philippines, and Pakistan, as well as countries in Africa. By 2000 immigration to the United States had returned to its 1900 volume, and the United States once again became a nation formed and transformed by immigrants.

Now in the early 21st century, American society once again finds itself locked in a debate over immigration and the role of immigrants in American society. To some, the new immigrants have seemed unwilling or unable to assimilate into American society, too committed to maintaining their transnational connections, and too far removed from core American values. As in past eras, some critics of contemporary immigrants believe that the newcomers take jobs away from Americans and put undue burdens on the educational, welfare, and health care systems. Many participants in the debate consider a large number of illegal immigrants to pose a threat to the society's basic structure.

The immigrants, however, have supporters who point out that each new immigrant wave inspired fear, suspicion, and concern by Americans—including the children and grandchildren of earlier immigrants—and that Americans claimed, wrongly, that each group of newcomers would somehow not fit in and would remain wedded to their old and foreign ways. So too advocates of immigration and most historians of immigration argue that immigrants enrich the United States, in large measure because they provide valuable services to the nation.

In every era of U.S. history, from colonial times in the 17th century through the early 21st century, women and men from around the world have opted for the American experience. They arrived as foreigners, bearers of languages, cultures, and religions that at times seemed alien to America's essential core. Over time, as ideas about U.S. culture changed, the immigrants and their descendants simultaneously built ethnic communities and participated in American civic life, contributing to the nation as a whole.

> *"To deny the ban on immigration because it has exceptions is like denying Alcohol Prohibition because it allowed communion wine."*

# It Is Virtually Impossible to Come to the United States to Live and Work Legally

*David J. Bier*

*In the following viewpoint, David Bier points to a historical moment in the twentieth century when America's open-door policy to immigrants was permanently "slam[med] shut." Showing the discrepancy between populations who are allowed into the country legally and those who must find illegal ways of entering, Bier argues that until legal immigration is allowed for larger and more diverse groups of people, illegal immigration will be a major battle that the American political establishment will continue to lose. Bier is an immigration policy analyst at the Cato Institute's Center for Global Liberty and Prosperity.*

As you read, consider the following questions:

1. According to Bier, when did America first "close its doors" and why?
2. Who are the vast amount of legal immigrants in the United States?
3. Why, according to the author, is illegal immigration such a problem in the United States today?

The United States has a de facto ban on immigration. We can debate about whether this prohibition is necessary, but its existence is undeniable. Other than a few exceptions for family members, refugees, and the highly-educated, it is virtually impossible to come to the United States to live and work legally.

Historically, America held its doors open to all. But in the 1920s, a coalition of unions, progressives, and eugenicists combined to slam them shut. Within a year of passing Alcohol Prohibition, America also banned almost all forms of immigration, cutting immigration by nearly 80 percent.

Alcohol regained its legal status, but immigration never quite recovered.

Today, the government lets in almost a million immigrants each year, but this impressive-sounding number misses the entire legal, historical, and global context of our immigration system. We must compare it to the number who would come if only they could do so legally—and the reality is that most types of immigration are entirely prohibited. To deny the ban on immigration because it has exceptions is like denying Alcohol Prohibition because it allowed communion wine.

The half million people apprehended at the border each year and the 11 million unauthorized immigrants in the country are the clear evidence of this prohibition. The massive immigration underground points to an obvious yet largely ignored fact: If there was a legal way for them to come, they would have taken it. But, trouble is, one doesn't exist.

The drastic shortage of visas is evident in the unbelievably long wait times for permanent residency. For certain categories, the wait is decades. For employment-based visas, certain Indian and Chinese workers will wait more than a decade. For Mexico, three different family-based categories have wait times over 18 years. There's northward of 4.3 million people in these lines alone.

Yet these impossible lines hide a deeper problem: most would-be immigrants have no line to stand in at all.

The reality is this: 92 percent of legal immigrants are either 1) immediate family members of US citizens or permanent residents, 2) refugees or asylees, or 3) college graduates—and over 80 percent of those needed an advanced degree or at least $500,000 to invest in projects in the United States.

This leaves less than 65,000 visas for everyone else. More than two-thirds of these come through a lottery system for which 11 million people applied last year. People in most of the largest countries in the world, including India, China, and Mexico, aren't even eligible to apply.

This legal flow amounts to barely 7 percent of the average number of immigrants apprehended at the border each year since 2004 (and, of course, that doesn't count those who crossed successfully, or those who entered and overstayed their visas, or those who would come if there was a legal opportunity). For people without a college degree or a close American relative, the Statue of Liberty's "Golden Door" is almost completely shut.

Meanwhile, PhDs, scientists, movie stars, pro-athletes, and other elites have a number of different work visas available to them. These allow them to live and work year-round in the United States.

By contrast, there is no work visa that allows lesser-skilled laborers to live and work year-round in this country. Unsurprisingly, this lesser-skilled demographic is disproportionately represented in the illegal population, 85 percent of whom lack a college degree.

Another reason we know that illegal immigration is being driven by the lack of a legal alternative is because of what happened when the government allowed foreign workers to come and go legally.

Thanks to a fluke of history, America had a brief period when it experimented with freer migration between the United States and Mexico. In the 1950s and '60s, the Bracero guest worker program let in about 5 million Mexican farmworkers. From 1956 to 1965, when the program was at its height, the number of unauthorized immigrants at the border averaged just 41,000, compared to over 436,000 a year in the prior decade.

After it was terminated in 1966 by another union-led coalition, illegal immigration never again fell to such low levels—not even for a single year, let alone an entire decade. By the 1980s, a million or more immigrants were routinely being caught by Border Patrol every year.

Supporters of the ban on immigration will say that America is at its breaking point, that we're overwhelmed, that we can't "handle" any more immigrants. But this fear is groundless: As a share of its population, America admitted four times as many immigrants each year in the early 1900s as it did in 2014. For a century from 1830-1929, immigration was twice as high as a share of the population as it was in the last two decades.

In absolute terms, America admits more immigrants than any other country, but relative to its size, US immigration levels are far lower than many Western countries. Controlling for population, Canada, Australia, and New Zealand all have higher levels of immigration than America today—even as high as the United States in the early 20th century—and they have not collapsed into chaos or poverty.

Immigration prohibition is real. Millions of people cross the border illegally (and thousands of businesses hire them illegally) for the same reason bootleggers had to brew booze in bathtubs. And, for the same reasons we repealed Alcohol Prohibition, we should also finally end America's ban on immigration.

> *"The rich, especially from countries such as Russia and China, are also leaving their home countries, but they are not faced with fences and rejection but welcomes and encouragement."*

# The Super-Rich Skirt Quotas and Closed Borders

*John Rennie Short*

*In the following viewpoint, John Rennie Short examines the recent phenomenon of countries trying to recruit wealthy immigrants inside their borders. This has been done by multiple countries in multiple ways, although Canada was at the forefront of the movement. In the European Union (EU), several countries even instituted a plan to allow the wealthy to pay approximately one million dollars in order to become EU citizens. However, as Short notes, this has not provided the economic benefits that these countries initially expected and, thus, should be scrapped. Short is a professor at the School of Public Policy at the University of Maryland, Baltimore County.*

As you read, consider the following questions:

1. How have some countries, like Canada, actively tried to "recruit" wealthy immigrants?
2. Do you think it makes economic sense for countries to try to attract wealthy immigrants into their borders? Why or why not?
3. What do you think about the idea of "cash for citizenship," or paying a hefty price for legal entrance into a country?

The mass media are filled with images of desperate refugees struggling to escape civil unrest. But it is not only the poor and the displaced who are on the move. The rich, especially from countries such as Russia and China, are also leaving their home countries, but they are not faced with fences and rejection but welcomes and encouragement.

A review of these policies highlights the dramatic differences between rich and poor when it comes to immigration. It also reveals the dubious economic benefits of catering to the super-rich.

## Cheapening citizenship?

Canada was the first rich country to go after the wealthy. Under its Immigrant Investor Program, first introduced in 1989, foreign nationals could gain residency in Canada by loaning (Canadian) $800,000 interest-free to any of the provinces for five years. The program was very attractive first to wealthy people from Hong Kong and then mainland China, as it was a relatively cheap method to gain residence in a secure, safe country with generous social benefits. More than 130,000 individuals entered Canada through this program. Vancouver became such a popular destination that locals refer to it as Hongcouver.

While the program was a boon to wealthy Chinese, it was seen increasingly in Canada as a too-cheap selling of their citizenship with negative effects on property markets by raising prices. When the program was cancelled in February 2014, it had

59,000 pending applicants, 45,000 from mainland China. At its peak in 2005, the program was responsible for almost 11% of the roughly 250,000 immigrants allowed into the country each year.

The UK has a Tier 1 investor visa for those from outside the European Economic Area (EEA) and Switzerland willing to invest one million British pounds in UK government bonds and UK-registered companies. It is a fast-track system that provides a visa decision within three weeks and allows you to bring immediate family members, still spend up to six months outside the UK and gain an easy path to full citizenship: a sweet deal. Applications run, on average, about 600 a year. A recent review concluded that the entry "fee" was too low, most of the money was invested in government bonds for which there is no lack of demand, and the greatest impact was on the London property market, raising prices beyond the reach of the locals.

Since 1990, the US has an employment-based program tailored for the wealthy entitled EB5. Under this program, 10,000 visas each year are reserved for investors to receive permanent residence status if they invest at least US$1 million (only $500,000 in high unemployment and rural areas) in a commercial enterprise that employs at least 10 full-time US workers.

Studies by trade groups estimate that the program contributed $3.39 billion to US GDP and resulted in 42,000 jobs in fiscal year 2012, while a more critical review of the EB5 program came to the conclusion that the visas are too cheap, the program is badly run and the bulk of the money goes to already overheated real estate markets.

An investigation by The New York Times documented the case of a 34-story glass tower in the middle of affluent Manhattan that was classified, through selective and creative use of census statistics, as a an area of high unemployment.

The total cost of the building was $750 million, with one-fifth coming from foreign investors seeking green cards through the EB5 program. More than four out of every five applicants of the 8,500 foreign investors now come from mainland China.

## Competition for the super-rich

Other countries with favored immigration policies for the wealthy include Australia, with its Significant Investor Visa introduced in 2012, popularly known as the "golden ticket," and Singapore's Global Investor Program. Malaysia has a "Malaysia's My Second Home" program tailored to rich retirees.

Much of Europe now counts as a single territorial unit in terms of freedom of movement and capital mobility. Some countries use their privileged position as entry points to sell access and citizenship.

In Latvia, for example, anyone who buys property worth at least 50,000 Lats (US$96,000) in provincial cities, and 100,000 Lats (US$192,000) in Riga, receives a five-year residency permit that allows them access to other countries in Europe. Since 2012, Portugal has a "golden visa" guaranteeing two-year residence in return for a 500,000 euro investment in real estate investment or a one million euro investment that creates 30 jobs. By March 2014, 542 visas were issued, with 433 going to Chinese applicants. In 2013, Spain and Greece adopted similar programs for real estate investments of 500,000 euros and 250,000 euros, respectively. The same year Hungary gave a residence permit in return for an investment of 250,000 euros and a payment to "partners" of the government for at least 40,000 euros. This is the same Hungary that has sought at times to block the flow of refugees from Syria and Iraq in recent weeks.

Malta proposed an Individual Investor Program that offered citizenship for a straight fee of 650,000 euros. After heavy criticism both domestically and from European partners that the program was effectively selling European citizenship, the program was placed on hold, and then in November 2013 a revised program offered citizenship in return for 1,150,000 euros.

Indeed, the competition for the rich is creating a downward pressure on the price of entry. In 2012, Portugal offered 500,000 euros for residency; the next year, Greece asked for only 250,000 euros.

## Trickle-down effect?

Even as rich countries review their policies, there is one thing that's quite clear: the rich are on the move, and more states want to attract them. But does it make economic sense to offer financial incentives to attract them?

One of the claims for those who promote and support a "cash for citizenship" approach is that it provides benefits to the country, such as increased investment and new jobs. However, the countries courting the rich already have lots of willing investors, and few jobs can be directly related to the programs. There is no shortage of foreign investors for Manhattan office blocks, even without the extra allure of a green card. Most official reviews now come to the conclusion that the programs, hastily conceived in the rush to attract the newly wealthy citizens of Russia, China and other countries, are too cheap with few benefits for the host countries.

In the US, authorization of the EB5 program, aimed at luring wealthy immigrants, runs out on September 30. The reauthorization tries to address the existing shortcomings with a wide-ranging reform of the initial program.

But despite the proposed changes and Congress' transparent attempt to wrap it up as a job creation and investment promotion, as the data clearly show, it is the selling of citizenship for a program with very limited benefits to the nation. It is a program that deserves to die.

> "*Even maintaining current immigration levels or instituting small liberalizations of American immigration policy may be threatened by what happened in Boston and similar immigrant-connected terrorism, let alone their negative impact on the push for open borders.*"

# Open Borders Would Help Protect the United States

*Joel Newman*

*In the following viewpoint, Joel Newman argues that lifting restrictions on immigration could actually benefit counterterrorism efforts. Newman examines how terrorist attacks perpetrated by Muslim immigrants, in particular, might harm activists' call for open borders and concludes that these terrorist attacks could create a punishing cycle for immigrants. Ironically, he contends, this works against US counterterrorism efforts, making further attacks more likely. Newman is a blogger at Open Borders who is also completing a book on the subject.*

As you read, consider the following questions:

1. Why might open borders actually help counterterrorism efforts?
2. What is the "availability bias" and how does it apply to immigration?
3. What do you think about open borders? Might there be any potential negatives?

I assume that other open borders supporters cringed, as I did, when it was reported that the suspects in the Boston bombings were immigrants. For some people, the Boston atrocity appears to have reinforced fears that immigrants could be terrorists. A man interviewed in a Philadelphia suburb said, "I'm a little more of an extremist now after what happened in Boston... I think we should just stop letting people in." Even maintaining current immigration levels or instituting small liberalizations of American immigration policy may be threatened by what happened in Boston and similar immigrant-connected terrorism, let alone their negative impact on the push for open borders.

Concerns about the connection between immigrants and terrorism involve Muslim immigrants. The Boston suspects were Muslims and may have been inspired by religious extremism to carry out the attacks. The Bipartisan Policy Center reports that the U.S. has "a domestic terrorist problem involving immigrant and indigenous Muslims as well as converts to Islam." (9/10/10, Bipartisan Policy Center, Assessing the Terrorist Threat, page 31) Even some open borders advocates seem uncertain if an open borders policy should apply to Muslim immigrants. In the site's background page on terrorism, Vipul paraphrases a view (not necessarily his own): "[F]or those who believe that Islamic immigration to the United States poses a unique threat, this may be a reason to maintain present restrictions on immigration from Islamic countries and self-identified Muslims from other countries."

Muslim immigration would increase with open borders, and some of these additional immigrants could become terrorists.

However, especially after situations like Boston (and there have been others), open borders supporters should explain how open borders could actually help protect the U.S. from terrorism and that open borders should be available to all individual immigrants, regardless of religion, so long as they pose no terrorist threat. Vipul has collected some of these arguments. My vision of open borders and that of a number of other supporters does involve keeping out potential terrorists through security screenings at the border. So one argument notes that, unlike our current restrictionist policy which devotes considerable resources and focus on keeping out unauthorized immigrants seeking to work in the U.S., resources under an open borders policy could be focused on screening out terrorists. Another argument is that the free movement of people between countries could lead to the spreading of ideas contrary to those which inspire terrorism; immigrants who move between the U.S. or other western countries and their native countries would share values such as individual rights, tolerance, and democracy with their compatriots who remain in the native countries. A third argument is that if terrorism grows out of weak economies in native countries, the free movement of people from those countries and the resulting economic benefit to those countries (through remittances and immigrants returning to their native country to establish new businesses) could help prevent terrorism.

There is another reason open borders could help combat terrorism. Kevin Johnson, author of *Opening the Floodgates*, notes that "carefully crafted immigration enforcement is less likely to frighten immigrant communities—the very communities whose assistance is essential if the United States truly seeks to successfully fight terrorism." (page 35) Without the fear of being the targets of immigration enforcement, immigrants would be more likely to cooperate with authorities in identifying individuals who are potential terrorists in the U.S. and assist with efforts against terrorist groups abroad. This would fit with the government's strategy to gain the cooperation of Muslims in the U.S. in addressing terrorism. Quintan Wiktorowicz, a national security staff member in the White House, notes in a discussion on an administration plan to fight terrorism in the U.S. that "Muslim communities and Muslims in the United States are not the problem, they are the solution. And that's the message we plan to take to those particular communities in addressing at least al-Qaida inspired radicalization of violent extremism…"

For the effort abroad, Nathan Smith suggests that "emigrants from Islamic countries could provide a valuable resource for the intelligence services of the West in their fight against Islamic terrorism." Open borders would presumably increase the number of immigrants from countries that have been sources of terrorism against the U.S., such as Pakistan, Afghanistan, and Yemen. Some of these immigrants could provide the cultural and language skills which would bolster our intelligence resources and help America stay safe from future attacks. Indeed, our intelligence agencies have often lacked agents who could infiltrate groups that threaten the U.S. (In an article in the *Atlantic Monthly* in the summer of 2001, Reuel Marc Gereht quoted a former CIA operative as saying "The CIA probably doesn't have a single truly qualified Arabic speaking officer of Middle Eastern background who can play a believable Muslim fundamentalist…" (pages 38-42, July/August 2001))

In addition to articulating the potential benefits of open borders to stopping terrorism, open borders advocates must emphasize that most Muslims are peaceful and should be allowed to immigrate. Philippe Legrain, author of *Immigrants: Your Country Needs Them*, warns "we should not fall into the trap of thinking that Muslims are a uniform and separate community whose identity is wholly defined by their religion, still less an inevitably hostile or violent one." (page 304) He notes that Muslims come from many different countries, each with their own traditions, and, like other religious groups, some are religious, some not. "There are feminist Muslims, gay Muslims and Muslims who reject their faith." (page 304) In addition, "only a small minority of Muslims are fundamentalist," and only a tiny number of fundamentalists are terrorists. (page 305) There are over 2.5 million Muslims living in the U.S., about two thirds of whom are immigrants, but very few are involved in terrorism. The Bipartisan Policy Center reports that in 2009 "at least 43 American citizens or residents aligned with Sunni militant groups or their ideology were charged or convicted of terrorism crimes in the U.S. or elsewhere, the highest number in any year since 9/11." (Page 5 of this report ) Mr. Legrain explains that "the threat of Islamic terrorism is a reason for increased vigilance, surveillance and scrutiny; it is not reason for limiting immigration."

Nathan Smith has noted that when dramatic events occur, such as an act of terrorism by immigrants or a plane crash, people often overestimate the frequency of such events, a phenomenon called "availability bias." This mental overreaction to "extremely unrepresentative events" makes people attribute more importance to the events than they deserve. This dynamic suggests that open borders supporters have a lot of work to do convincing the public that most Muslims who want to immigrate pose no threat and that open borders may actually help in the fight against terrorism.

> "[The border wall's] location is prima facie evidence that the 'immigration issue' is really a euphemism for keeping poor brown-skinned people out of the US—as well as creating a 'practice' zone for protecting American economic and political interests in Mexico and Central America."

# The "Immigration Issue" Is a Euphemism for Keeping Poor Brown-Skinned People Out of the United States

## Mark Karlin

*In the following viewpoint, Mark Karlin examines how different groups of people are treated differently by the US immigration system. In particular, he examines the psychological reasons why so much political rhetoric has been dedicated to constructing a wall between the United States and Mexico. Karlin posits that the only reason there is a physical southern border is because of racial anxieties between white Americans and poorer "brown-skinned" immigrants. The wall is a costly and ineffective psychological game, then, to ease these racial tensions. Karlin is the editor of BuzzFlash at Truthout, where he has interviewed political activists and written many articles about the Iraq War.*

"The Border Wall: The Last Stand at Making the US a White Gated Community," by Mark Karlin, Truthout, March 11, 2012. Reprinted by permission.

As you read, consider the following questions:

1. Karlin states that the border wall with Mexico is a project for reasons of "psychological reassurance"? Do you agree or disagree?

2. What are some of the physical barriers to constructing a physical wall between the US and Mexico?

3. Why is the wall a symbol of "racial anxiety," according to the author?

The physical Mexican-American wall starts as a newly fortified metal barrier extending 300 feet into the warm, balmy waters of Southern California and ends up some 2,000 miles later just east of Brownsville, Texas. But it would be wrong to think of it as continuous, because only about a third of that distance has some form of visible barrier running like a scar across the US border with Mexico.

The origins of the billions of dollars spent on the largely symbolic, highly visible wall really starts much farther north with US organizations and people advocating for a white political power structure, groups like one recently represented at the Conservative Political Action Conference (CPAC), which contend that a multicultural society is a danger to America. The wall also begins with the efforts of states like Arizona to erase Mexican-American culture from the textbooks in state schools, even in districts where the vast majority of students are of Mexican descent. It begins with Republicans such as Mitt Romney welcoming the endorsements of white nationalists who campaign at his side. It starts with draconian Alabama's, Arizona's and Georgia's harsh anti-"immigrant" laws that are spreading to many state legislatures, born of racism and self-serving industry lobbies such as privatized prisons.

The construction of the "barrier" wall—accompanying large-scale militarization (the Border Patrol, Immigration and Customs

Enforcement, the FBI, the Drug Enforcement Agency, the FBI, the military etc.)—is on America's southern border, and there is meaning in that. Its location is prima facie evidence that the "immigration issue" is really a euphemism for keeping poor brown-skinned people out of the US—as well as creating a "practice" zone for protecting American economic and political interests in Mexico and Central America.

## Migration Is Not About Opportunism; It's About Survival

The overwhelming majority of migrants from Mexico who seek undocumented entrance to US are desperate, not gold diggers. They are often victims of an indigenous subsistence agricultural and rural economy that is disappearing, due to NAFTA and US subsidies of American farmers, who can sell for lower competitive prices "south of the border." Often facing an arduous, dangerous trip up from southern Mexico or Central America, they are willing to confront possible death in the deserts, sometimes relying on treacherous "coyotes" (guides), who claim to offer them safe passage to the US in return for exorbitant fees, and professional criminals, who abuse and steal from them as they head to the border.

The strong anti-"immigration" laws of many states and the harsh enforcement of the federal government, however, may be backfiring, because migrants in dire economic need will work for very little under squalid conditions—and, therefore, are a valued "commodity." A 2011 Christian Science Monitor article notes that in Alabama, "farmers fearing a labor shortage are protesting recent immigration laws they say are too harsh, forcing undocumented workers to flee to prevent deportation." The farmers say, "US workers are unwilling to endure the rigorous conditions of farm work and that" local farmers may go bankrupt. But the proponents of white American exceptionalism have no tolerance for a multicultural society, even if such a stance hurts the US agricultural (and other low-pay labor areas) financial penchant for labor exploitation.

## Expats and Immigrants

In the lexicon of human migration there are still hierarchical words, created with the purpose of putting white people above everyone else. One of those remnants is the word "expat."

What is an expat? And who is an expat? According to Wikipedia, "an expatriate (often shortened to expat) is a person temporarily or permanently residing in a country other than that of the person's upbringing. The word comes from the Latin terms ex ('out of') and patria ('country, fatherland')."

Defined that way, you should expect that any person going to work outside of his or her country for a period of time would be an expat, regardless of his skin colour or country. But that is not the case in reality; expat is a term reserved exclusively for western white people going to work abroad.

Africans are immigrants. Arabs are immigrants. Asians are immigrants. However, Europeans are expats because they can't be at the same level as other ethnicities. They are superior. Immigrants is a term set aside for 'inferior races.'

**"Why are white people expats when the rest of us are immigrants?" by Mawuna Remarque Koutonin, Guardian News and Media Limited, March 13, 2015.**

## Can the US Wall Off a Culturally Diverse Society?

"It seems to me that the notion of a literal wall between Mexico and the US signifies both the physical and existential threat that many white Americans perceive from those with darker skin," Timothy Wise, an expert on how the fear of power being shared in America by its diverse population is creating racial anxiety in many whites, told Truthout. "On the one hand, there is the sense that such persons are literally going to harm us—through crime, the mythical overuse of taxpayer funded services or some other thing—and on the other, the larger paranoia that they pose a threat to the cultural and social survival of America as 'we have known it.'"

Recently, I stood in downtown Brownsville on a sliver of land ironically called "Hope Park." I read about how ferries used to cross the narrow stretch of the Rio Grande there, making it easier for the citizens of both nations to move unimpeded from one country to another. Instead, as I looked toward Mexico, there was a high fence of vertical bars in front of me, one of the more "attractive" versions of the wall, which varies in construction design from location to location (in some places it is just corrugated sheets of metal and in others it may be three consecutive physical barriers). "Hope," the celebration of a blended heritage and opportunity, had literally been fenced off from this wedge of land.

The border wall divides people of common culture and heritage, including not just Mexicans, but also Native Americans. Just to the west of Brownsville, is the town of El Calaboz, an indigenous community where Lipan Apache, Tlaxcalteca, Nahua, Comanche and Basque colonists have had extensive interactions since the Spanish colonial era. Margo Tamez, an assistant professor at the University of British Columbia—who holds a cross-appointment in indigenous studies and gender and women's studies—grew up there, learning the history of native oppression from her Lipan Apache elders.

Tamez, like Wise, views the wall as a physical symbol of oppression of peoples who are not white. Talking with Tamez, one gets a sense of the richness of her heritage and what a toll that squashing out diversity—instead of embracing it—takes. Tamez wants her lineage to be clear. She is a member of the Lipan Apache Band of Texas, or in their language, of the Konitsaaíí ndé ("Big Water Clan") and Cúelcahén ("Tall Grass People Clan"), the southernmost of the Athabascan peoples, who stretch from British Columbia to Tamaulipas and Coahuila, Mexico. The Athabascan peoples span three borders, as does their common culture.

Indigenous peoples along the Texas border wall were also the first peoples, according to Tamez, with whom the Spanish colonial government entered into land grants. Tamez's mother, Eloisa García Tamez (whose family was granted a plot in 1767 by Spain), is lead plaintiff in an ongoing lawsuit against the federal government claiming the wall's construction is a violation of Texas land law;

Crown land grant and riparian laws; treaties among Lipan Apaches, Texas and the US; and international law.

Tamez told Truthout that the wall is representative of the "genealogy of hate and an entrenched worldview which is based upon contempt and disdain for indigenous peoples globally. The wall represents the legacy of that particular world view—a 'deathscape' which is a means of continuing to colonize through mechanization of cages and walls at a vast scale, and which demands its own existence through indigenous peoples' containment in open air prisons in our homelands, our traditional territories." Tamez maintains a web site about the Apache struggle for indigenous rights and lands in which she writes, "Apachean peoples still have a deep sense of being cloistered, imprisoned, contained, detained, and displaced in fractured ways by those visibly militarized architectural features on our territorial spaces."

## Lower Rio Grand Valley Is a Cage for Many

Indeed, the lower Rio Grand Valley is literally a cage for many. If you travel north by car on the only highway out of Brownsville, Route 77, after about an hour, you come to an immigration checkpoint. If you are undocumented, you will likely be apprehended here and deported, unless you have some foolproof, forged papers. If you are an American citizen (of brown skin color) and are suspected of being an "illegal alien," you may be searched and harassed. In short, without a passport or a driver's license, many residents of the lower Rio Grande Valley are trapped.

Oddly, not only does the wall currently only run along a portion of the border with Mexico, but there are often literally holes (cutouts) in it. Some of the lower Rio Grande Valley residents involved in a losing battle against wall construction say that these gaps prove that its construction is for symbolic political purposes. The Department of Homeland Security (DHS) has countered that there is an "electronic high-tech" wall that covers the cutouts, which were allegedly built so that the ubiquitous white Border

Patrol vans, emergency vehicles, farm workers and residents could access the south side of the wall.

Why would people need to access the south side of the wall? Because of a combination of factors—including an international flood plain agreement and political influence that was brought to bear on where the wall was built—there are US residents and agricultural fields south of the wall. Remember that the barricade is supposedly being constructed in order to protect Americans from illegal immigrants and narco trade violence. The people living or working on the "other side" of the wall, if you accept the official version of the intent behind its construction, have been abandoned to marauders.

The Brownsville area home of family farm owner Tim Loop ended up on the south side of the wall, according to an article in Texas Monthly (reprinted in The New York Times). Loop's horizon view now consists of "imposing sections of 15- to-18- foot-high rust-colored steel bars, some less than 400 feet from Mr. Loop's front porch." But what most concerns Loop is that the DHS has plans to close the "cutouts" in the fence with keypad controlled gates.

"Mr. Loop wonders," Texas Monthly writes, "if possessing a secret pass code could make him a target for anyone desperate to gain access to the other side. This is, after all, a familiar area to desperate travelers."

"They tore down hundred-year-old trees to put up a fence," a neighbor of Loop said. "You think they care about how using a keypad is going to affect us?"

## Absurdities Do Arise

When a project as large as the wall takes place for reasons of psychological reassurance rather than for its officially stated purpose, absurdities do arise.

One morning, I drove over a humped ridge into the historic Fort Brown Memorial Golf Course, which appeared filled with seniors, all white from what I could see—a scene from a morning retirement community in Florida. Despite University of Texas at Brownsville efforts, the 18-hole course ended up on the south side of the wall—although the barrier was modified in appearance to cross the campus here as a low, chain-link fence with white brick posts and a driveway opening. I drove along what looked like an access road that serviced the links, when in no short time, I turned and saw someone putting up laundry. I was looking over the Rio Grande at Matamoros in Mexico—Brownsville's sister city.

Within a few seconds a Border Patrol van was racing toward me. After reviewing my media credentials and passport, the agent warned me to leave the area because it was "dangerous." I looked to my right and there was a foursome teeing off, just a few yards from the river.

Obviously. it wasn't too dangerous to golf. In fact, on a web site that features golf course reviews, one player at Fort Brown wrote, "this is a very scenic and historical course. It also is a place to enjoy—while you play, native birds and animals [abound]."

Yes, there are real issues of jobs being lost in the US, of narco violence and more. But a wall will not stop these problems; the loss of American jobs is primarily due to the shipment of the manufacturing sector to lower-cost countries, and the appetite in the US for illegal drugs will not be halted by a physical barrier. Time magazine reports on one of the latest narco evasions of the Mexican border wall (and the vast array of border enforcement strategies), the successful use of submarines manufactured in Colombia for the express purpose of drug transport. A multibillion industry is, like a global corporation, able to financially find a way of getting its product to market.

## Easing White Racial Anxiety at What Cost?

According to a 2011 New York Times (NYT) article, DHS had spent $21 million per mile to build a fence near San Diego (although the costs of construction in Texas are estimated to be lower). Estimates of building a full Mexican border fence range up to $40 billion dollars—and then there are several billion dollars in maintenance costs over the next few years. But Richard Cortez, the mayor of McAllen—just down the road (Route 83) west of Brownsville—told the NYT, "It is a winding river [the Rio Grande]. Where in the world are you going to put fencing? To propose that suggests ignorance of the border and the terrain."

Then what is the physical wall, whose continued construction became a big issue early on as part of the "immigration" debate among GOP candidates, for? In some ways, it's a political curtain that's a backdrop for appeasing racial resentment and job losses. It's the way of giving the illusion of an American-gated community for whites. But the wall is also tied into creating a military gateway into neighboring southern countries that need to be "stabilized" for purposes of low-cost labor and open markets. It's just that the wall is a prop, whereas the other law enforcement, intelligence agency and Pentagon initiatives on and around the border are deadly serious.

In that respect, the wall gives a false and expensive taxpayer-built sense of easing white racial anxiety. Complicated, cynical and dangerous cross currents are the real issues swirling along the border, including the lowest-cost labor goals of global corporations, and the hemispheric and narco policies of the United States government.

As Wise observes in his most recent book, "Dear White America: Letter to a New Minority," "the real problem is less about the distinction between documented and undocumented immigrants, and more about the mere fact of brown-skinned migration in the first place. Many of us simply don't want particular people, no matter the manner in which they come."

> *"Gender inequalities seep through immigration law in the United States, making women go through a different experience than men when attempting to gain a legal status in the U.S., a new study reveals."*

# US Immigration Law Treats Women and Men Differently

*Griselda Nevarez*

*In the following viewpoint, Griselda Nevarez uses a study conducted between 1998 and 2007 by Cecilia Menjivar and Olivia Salcido to spotlight gender disparity in immigration. According to the study, women experience gender biases when they try to pursue a legal status in the United States. While immigration law appears to be gender neutral, it can actively work against women, particularly because women are often viewed as "dependents" to their male relatives and are thus discriminated against. Men, on the other hand, are often viewed as the "primary breadwinners" or the economic agents in their households, giving them the power to receive visas for their whole family under the stipulation of family reunification. Nevarez is a journalist whose work has appeared in the* Guardian, *on MSNBC, and on NBC News.*

"U.S. Immigration Law Treats Women And Men Differently," by Griselda Nevarez, Times Internet Limited, May 6, 2013. Reprinted by permission of Griselda Nevarez, VOXXI.

As you read, consider the following questions:

1. What are some of the gender inequalities that "seep" through US immigration law?
2. What are the four different avenues through which women seek legal status in the US?
3. How can these different ways of becoming "legal" affect women differently than men?

Gender inequalities seep through immigration law in the United States, making women go through a different experience than men when attempting to gain a legal status in the U.S., a new study reveals.

"Immigration law, which on its face appears gender neutral, actually contains gender biases that create barriers for many women trying to gain legalization within the current immigration system," stated the authors of a study released last week by the Immigration Policy Center.

Cecilia Menjivar—a professor at Arizona State University—and Olivia Salcido—a researcher who studies law, immigration and domestic violence—spent more than a decade researching the experiences of women and men who go through the legalization process. From 1998 to 2007, they conducted 51 in-depth interviews in Arizona with immigrants originally from Mexico, El Salvador, Guatemala and Honduras.

The findings were surprising.

"We found that even laws written specifically to protect women, such as the Violence Against Women Act (VAWA), continued to play out in practice along gender-biased lines," Menjivar and Salcido wrote in the study.

They also found that the U.S. immigration system is not designed to recognize immigrant women's needs and circumstances. Additionally, they found that immigrant women are often presumed to be "dependents" while men are looked at as the primary breadwinners, which results in women and men having different experiences when they go through the legalization process.

## How gender shapes four avenues for legalization

In their study, the authors highlighted how gender shapes four different avenues through which women seek a legal status in the U.S.: employment-based visas, family reunification, the asylum process and a VAWA visa.

When it comes to applying for employment-based visas, many women, instead of applying as principle visa holders, rely on male relatives to petition for them to get such visas. This is because women often have domestic jobs, such as cleaning houses, that are not considered by U.S. immigration law as "high demand" jobs—a requirement to obtain an employment-based visa.

In addition, more men apply as principal visa holders when they seek employment-based visas because they have more opportunities than women to earn college degrees and acquire skills in their native countries. But even when women are highly skilled, they still find it difficult to gain employment-based visas, the study revealed.

Many women also rely on male relatives to petition for them through the family-based immigration process, which is the primary avenue through which women gain legal status in the U.S. Women rely on men because they are often seen as "dependents" even when they have jobs outside the home. Meanwhile, men are largely viewed as primary breadwinners and heads of households, making it easier and faster for them to gain legal status through family reunification.

Another option is to seek a visa through political asylum. Here, women struggle to convince decision-makers that certain political actions and opinions establish a threat in their countries of origin. The authors of the study explained this, stating that a woman who fears persecution because of her engagement in political activities—activities defined by her gender, such as providing shelter for guerrillas—may find it more difficult to prove that it's reasonable to fear persecution than it is for a male who has also engaged in "male-defined activities," such as joining a guerrilla army.

Many immigrant women also struggle to prove persecution even when they were politically persecuted and, as a result, targeted with death threats in their native countries. One problem that women run into is not keeping documents that would prove they went through potential dangers. Such was the case for Sara, an asylum seeker from El Salvador featured in the study. The request was denied because she and her husband didn't keep the papers that showed the written death threats sent to them. But, the study states that even if the couple would have kept the documents, Sara would have still been denied asylum because the threats were directed at her husband—even though she was also at risk.

Lastly, women also face obstacles when applying for protection under the Violence Against Women Act (VAWA), which allows immigrant women who are victims of domestic violence to self-petition or independently seek legal immigration status in the U.S. One obstacle women face is providing evidence, such as documents with their name and of the abuser, to prove they live with their abuser. This is a difficult requirement to meet if a woman's abuser is the main breadwinner and the bills are all under his name.

## Address gender biases in immigration law through reform

Menjivar and Salcido concluded their study calling for an immigration reform that includes a path to citizenship that is "open, affordable, and accessible to all immigrant women, including those whose work is unpaid (e.g., those in the care economy), and those employed in the informal economy."

They also called for a number of improvements that should be made to the legalization process, including adding more avenues for immigrant women to access the legalization process without having to rely on male relatives and on principal visa holders to petition on their behalf.

Emily Butera, senior program officer for the Migrant Rights and Justice Program at the Women's Refugee Commission, agreed on having an immigration reform that addresses the obstacles women face when they go through the legalization process in the U.S.

"The political reality is that if we are going to have a serious national conversation about immigration reform, we have to talk about immigrant women," Butera said in a conference call with reporters last week. "We've known that to be true for a long time now based on past experience, and the data that we have available to us."

She also noted that there are currently 5 million undocumented women who are living in the U.S. and could benefit from an immigration reform. She said that that statistic "tells us more than anything else that if we don't talk about accounting for the needs and lived experiences of immigrant women in immigration reform, we're going to be looking back on this immigration reform effort 10 years down the road and discover that we failed."

# Periodical and Internet Sources Bibliography

*The following articles have been selected to supplement the diverse views presented in this chapter.*

Monica Boyd and Elizabeth Grieco, "Women and Migration: Incorporating Gender into International Migration Theory," Migration Policy Institute, March 1, 2003. http://www .migrationpolicy.org/article/women-and-migration -incorporating-gender-international-migration-theory.

Eliot Brown, "Immigrant Investor Program for Poor Neighborhoods Benefits Rich Ones More, Study Shows," *Wall Street Journal*, October 19, 2016. http://www.wsj.com/articles/immigrant -investor-program-for-poor-neighborhoods-benefits-rich-ones -more-study-shows-1476917304.

The Center for Immigration Studies, "Immigrants in the United States: A Profile of America's Foreign-Born Population," The Center for Immigration Studies. http://cis.org/node/3876.

Charles Davis, "They're Only 'Illegals' If They're Brown," *Vice*, March 7, 2014. https://www.vice.com/en_us/article/theyre-only-illegals -if-theyre-brown.

*The Economist*, "No Country for Poor Men," March 1, 2014. http:// www.economist.com/news/britain/21597888-if-government -wants-sell-visas-it-should-make-more-money-them-no- country-poor.

Jeff Guo, "The Telling Way White Americans React to Pictures of Dark-Skinned Immigrants," *Washington Post*, January 12, 2016. https://www.washingtonpost.com/news/wonk/wp/2016/01/12 /the-telling-way-white-americans-react-to-pictures-of-dark -skinned-immigrants/?utm_term=.4b47fb637e17.

Kalyan Kumar, "Canada's Super Rich Immigration Program Draws Poor Response," *International Business Times*, July 28, 2015. http://www.ibtimes.com.au/canadas-super-rich-immigration -program-draws-poor-response-1457837.

Yael Ossowski, "The Difference Between Expats and Immigrants? It's Passports, Not Race," *PanamPost*, March 26, 2015. https:// panampost.com/yael-ossowski/2015/03/26/the-difference -between-expats-and-immigrants-its-passports-not-race.

Douglas Todd, "Gap Between Rich-Poor Immigrants Has Lessons for All Canadians," *Vancouver Sun*, January 18, 2011. http:// vancouversun.com/news/staff-blogs/gap-between-rich-poor -immigrants-has-lessons-for-all-canadians.

Sadhbh Walshe, "Justin Bieber Is Lucky He's Rich—Poor Immigrants Don't Get Off So Easy," *Alternet*, January 29, 2014. http://www .alternet.org/immigration/justin-bieber-lucky-hes-rich-poor -immigrants-dont-get-so-easy.

CHAPTER 2

# How Can We Reconcile Humanitarian and Security Concerns for Refugees and Immigrants?

# Chapter Preface

The discussion in the United States revolving around immigration changed drastically in light of the September 11, 2001, terrorist attacks. The perpetrators of these crimes arrived legally in the United States on either student or work visas. Many Americans clamored that their government was irresponsible in allowing these terrorists to enter the country without question. Thus began the age of increased security; biometric technology, in which people were tracked using their physical characteristics and past history; and tightened border controls. Some politicians, citizens, and organizations even advocated for those immigrants from Arab or Muslim countries to be blocked entry into the United States. Americans feared that background checks would not be sufficient enough to catch those whose sole purpose for entering the United States was to carry out attacks against American citizens.

Then, following the 2011 Arab Spring and the Syrian civil war, this debate intensified in light of the millions of refugees seeking protection from violence and famine. In 2014, the number of migrants displaced by war or famine reached 60 million, a number not seen since the end of World War II. We are indeed in a global period of crisis, where millions of people seek refuge from the violence and instability that claims their native countries. Within Europe and the United States, this caused great debates over the responsibility of countries to accept these refugees. Some politicians suggested that many of these refugees could indeed be Islamic fundamentalists and terrorists. Some governors, including New Jersey's Chris Christie, even went so far as to state that they would not resettle any refugees, even if they were children under the age of five. Critics of this stance noted that the region from which many refugees were fleeing had actually been stabilized by American foreign policy and, thus, the United States had a moral responsibility to resettle these refugees. They further noted that refugees were unlikely to be fundamentalists or terrorists, as they were fleeing from the effects of terrorism themselves, and that most terrorist attacks that had been carried out in recent years in the United States had actually been carried out by American citizens. This contentious debate continues to this day, and the use of extreme political rhetoric instead of facts and data further obfuscates the issue of how to balance humanitarian concerns with security concerns in the resettlement of refugees. This chapter explores the issue from all sides.

| "*The security threat posed by refugees in the United States is insignificant.*"

# Syrian Refugees Don't Pose a Security Threat

*Alex Nowrasteh*

*In the following viewpoint, Alex Nowrasteh uses in-depth statistical research to show that refugees do not, in fact, pose a security threat to the United States. This is due, in part, to the strenuous vetting system that the US uses. In fact, it would be easier for terrorists to attack the US in another way, rather than seeking to enter the US immigration system. It does not make sense, according to Nowrasteh, to turn away refugees due to a statistically insignificant security risk. Alex Nowrasteh is an immigration policy analyst at the Cato Institute's Center for Global Liberty and Prosperity.*

As you read, consider the following questions:

1. What are some differences between refugees and asylum seekers?
2. What are some of the most convincing data, in your opinion, that Nowrasteh uses to shore up his argument?
3. How are multistep security screenings for refugees conducted?

"Syrian Refugees Don't Pose a Serious Security Threat," by Alex Nowrasteh, Cato Institute, November 18, 2015. http://www.cato.org/blog/syrian-refugees-dont-pose-serious-security-threat. Licensed under CC-BY-NA-3.0.

O f the 859,629 refugees admitted from 2001 onwards, only three have been convicted of planning terrorist attacks on targets outside of the United States, and none was successfully carried out. That is one terrorism-planning conviction for every 286,543 refugees that have been admitted. To put that in perspective, about 1 in every 22,541 Americans committed murder in 2014. The terrorist threat from Syrian refugees in the United States is hyperbolically over-exaggerated and we have very little to fear from them because the refugee vetting system is so thorough.

The brutal terrorist attack in France last Friday reignited a debate over accepting refugees from Syria and the Middle East. A Syrian who applied for asylum could have been one of the attackers, although his passport was a forgery. (As of this writing, all identified attackers have been French or Belgian nationals.) Governors and presidential candidates have voiced opposition to accepting any Syrian refugees, while several bills in Congress could effectively end the program.

There are many differences between Europe's vetting of asylum seekers from Syria and how the United States screens refugees. The geographic distance between the United States and Syria allows our government to better vet those seeking to come here, while large numbers of Syrians who try to go to Europe are less carefully vetted. A lax security situation there does not imply a lax security situation here.

## The Differences between Refugees and Asylum Seekers

Much of the confusion over the security threat posed by refugees is over the term "refugee" itself. It's not yet clear how many foreign attackers in Paris entered Europe, but one or more may have entered disguised as asylum seekers.

In the United States, asylum seekers who show up at U.S. borders and ask to stay must show they have a well-founded fear of persecution due to their race, religion, nationality, membership in a particular social group, or their political opinion if they return to their country of origin. There is an application and investigation process, and the government often detains the asylum seeker during that process. But the investigation and vetting of the asylum seeker often take place while he is allowed inside of the United States. Many of the Syrians and others who have entered Europe are asylum seekers who are vetted through similar, less stringent security screens.

Refugees are processed from a great distance away and are more thoroughly vetted than asylum seekers as a result. In the United States, a refugee is somebody who is identified by the United Nations High Commissioner for Refugees (UNHCR) in a refugee camp. UNHCR does the first round of security checks on the refugee according to international treaties to which the United States is a party and refers some of those who pass the initial checks to the U.S. Refugee Admissions Program (USRAP). The referrals are then interviewed by a U.S. Citizenship and Immigration Services (USCIS) officer abroad. The refugee must be outside the United States, be of special humanitarian concern to the government, demonstrate persecution or fear of persecution due to race, religion, nationality, political opinion, or membership in a particular social group, and must not be firmly resettled in another country.

Because the refugee is abroad while the U.S. government checks their background, potential terrorist links, and their claims to refugee status, the vetting is a lot more thorough and can take up to two years for non-Syrians. For Syrians, the vetting can take about three years because of the heightened concerns over security.

Asylum seekers, on the other hand, face rigorous checks, but they are conducted while the asylum seeker is inside of the United States and not always while he is in a detention center. Syrians fleeing violence who come to the United States will be refugees, whereas many getting into Europe are asylum seekers. This crucial distinction shows that the United States is in a far better security situation vis-à-vis Europe on any potential terrorist threat from Syrians.

The distinction between asylum seekers and refugees is usually lost when discussing the security threat from refugees. The father of Boston Marathon bombers Tamerlan and Dzokhar Tsarnaev was granted asylum status, which conferred derivative asylum status on the children. None of the Tsarnaevs were ever refugees.

Both Tamerlan and Dzokhar were children when they were admitted through their parents' asylum claims. They did not adopt a radical interpretation of Islam or start plotting a terrorist attack until years after coming here. Their case does not reveal flaws in the refugee vetting process. There were some other terrorist attacks in the early 1990s from applicants for asylum status, but none of them were actual refugees.

## Security Screenings for Refugees

Deputy State Department Spokesman Mark Toner called the security checks for refugees "the most stringent security process for anyone entering the United States." Coming here as a refugee requires numerous security and background checks that are more intense and invasive than for other migrants or visitors—which is partly why refugees have not successfully carried out terrorist attacks on U.S. soil (three have been convicted of attempting to carry out attacks abroad, there was one borderline case from a refugee who entered in 1997, and at least one other for a refugee who entered prior to 2001).

The first step for a refugee is to arrive and register in a UNHCR refugee camp outside of Syria. The UNHCR then refers those who pass the first stage of vetting to the U.S. government refugee process (as described above). The National Counterterrorism Center, the Terrorist Screening Center, the Department of Defense, the FBI, Department of Homeland Security, and the State Department use biometrics and biographical information gleaned through several interviews of the refugee and third-party persons who know him or could know him to make sure applicants really are who they claim to be, to evaluate their security risk, and to investigate whether they are suspected of criminal activity or terrorism. Numerous medical checks are also performed. During this entire screening process, which takes about three years for Syrians, the refugee has to wait in the camp. If there is any evidence that the refugee is a security threat, he or she is not allowed to come to the United States.

Refugee security screenings go beyond weeding out actual terrorists but also seek to identify those who provided material support to them. This material support standard is very elastic and weeds out many otherwise deserving refugees. Human Rights First claims that under current interpretations of the material support standard, Syrians would be turned away under all of these circumstances:

- A family who, while their residential neighborhood was being bombed by government forces, sheltered a wounded opposition fighter in their home;
- A boy who, after his father was killed, was recruited by opposition forces and, after serving with them for a time, left the conflict to join his mother and younger siblings in a neighboring country;
- The owner of a food stand in a neighborhood under opposition control from whom opposition fighters bought falafel sandwiches.

A refugee from Burundi was detained by DHS for 20 months for materially supporting a terrorist group because rebels beat him up, stole $4 from him, and took his lunch (it's unclear from the story, but he might have been an asylum seeker). Many good candidates for resettlement in the United States are turned down for these silly reasons.

## How Many Refugees Make It Here?
## How Many Are Syrians?

The UNHCR annually refers less than one percent of all refugees for resettlement. In 2014, they referred a mere 103,890 to all resettlement nations. That year, the United States accepted 69,933 refugees, or about 0.5 percent of the total number of all refugees in the world, but over 67 percent of all those referred by UNHCR.

In 2015, the United States has accepted only 1,682 Syrian refugees, or 0.042 percent of the 4,045,650 registered Syrian refugees. Only one out of every 2,405 Syrian refugees in a camp was resettled in the United States in 2015.

## Evaluating the Risk

Few ISIS soldiers or other terrorists are going to spend at least three years in a refugee camp for a 0.042 percent chance of entering the United States when almost any other option to do so is easier, cheaper, and quicker.

If the United States still takes in 10,000 Syrian refugees in 2016, and the number of refugees rises to 4.5 million, a mere 0.22 percent of them—one out of every 450—will be resettled in the United States. That number is still so small and the process so well monitored that potential terrorists are unlikely to see the refugee system as a viable way to enter the United States.

Foreign-born terrorists tend to enter on student visas, tourist visas, business visas, or have asylum applications pending, or are lawful permanent residents. All non-immigrant or immigrant categories face fewer security and background screenings than refugees do.

Of the 859,629 refugees who have entered the United States since 2001, three have been convicted for planning a terrorist attack abroad and exactly zero have perpetrated domestic attack—that's one conviction for every 286,543 refugees admitted. Focusing on the 735,920 refugees from Africa, Asia, the Middle East, and South Asia, that's one conviction for every 245,307 refugees admitted. Just to hammer the point home, these are convictions for planning terrorist attacks abroad, not for carrying out actual terrorist attacks in the United States.

In 2015, 53 percent of the Syrians admitted were men, while only 41.5 percent of those men were between the ages of 14 and 40. Of all the Syrian refugees in that year, only 22.3 percent of them were men between the ages of 14 and 40. Terrorism-related convictions are almost always of men, so any risk-assessment should note the small number of men in the applicable age ranges.

# CONNECTIONS BETWEEN
# IMMIGRATION AND TERRORISM?

Some restrictionists have made arguments that relate the problems of terrorism (such as the 9/11 terrorist attacks in 2001) with illegal immigration in the United States. There are some legitimate concerns about terrorism and immigration (as well as tourist visas) on the whole. But illegal immigration along the southern US border is not a contributor to terrorism. Some of the reasons are outlined below.

- Empirically, the case is simply false. Foreigners who've carried out terrorist attacks have entered the United States legally on immigrant, non-immigrant work/study, or tourist visas. While some of them may have been "illegal" in the sense of overstaying their visas, this is a qualitatively different problem than border crossing.
- Getting a tourist visa remains considerably easier than getting an immigrant or work/study visa. This point was made by David Friedman in a blog post titled Immigration and Terrorism.
- In recent history, most terrorism in the United States has been motivated by certain Islamist ideologies. Most illegal immigrants who cross the border to the United States come from Mexico and Latin America, where Catholicism is the main religion. Radical Islam has, if anything, less of a stronghold in these countries than in the United States.
- Apprehension rates for people attempting to cross the southern US border are quite high—about 25-50%. While this apprehension rate may be acceptable for drug mules and economic migrants who are desperate to improve their condition, it is not acceptable for people who wish to plan terrorist attacks, because they would get detained and fingerprinted and their network may get infiltrated. This point was made by Jeremy Shapiro, a national security expert at the Brookings Institution.

Let's assume, for the sake of argument, that individual Syrian refugees are three times as likely to attempt terrorism in the United States than non-Syrian refugees because they are super-radicalized and very good at hiding it while waiting for years in refugee camps for their chance to strike. Assuming this fantasy is true, the United States can expect to convict a single Syrian refugee for attempting a terrorist attack for every 95,514 of them allowed in as refugees. There are many more convictions for attempted terrorism than successful terrorist attacks. Without even attempting to estimate the damage caused by such hypothetical terrorist attacks, it's clear that the present political panic and calls for a moratorium on refugee admissions from Syria are totally unwarranted.

This situation may be different in Europe, where 681,713 Syrian asylum seekers have sought refuge since the beginning of their civil war in 2011. So far, one of them may have participated in the Paris terrorist attack, and that is far from clear.

John Mueller and Mark G. Stewart have been critical of counterterrorism agencies that "simply identify a source of harm and try to do something about it, rather than systematically thinking about the likely magnitude of harm caused by a successful terrorist attack, the probability of that attack occurring, and the amount of risk reduction that can be expected from counterterrorism efforts." These criticisms could easily apply to the U.S. refugee vetting process. To my knowledge, there has been no systematic evaluation of the costs and benefits of this refugee vetting process. The marginal costs of outlays and security procedures may exceed the marginal benefits, but that means we have even less to fear from those refugees admitted even if the price we pay for that safety is irrationally high.

There is also a risk from not letting in more Syrian refugees that policymakers should consider. Syrians could languish in refugee camps for years or decades to come unless the Turkish government suddenly becomes more classically liberal and hands out millions of work permits. There is one clear lesson from the limited academic literature on this issue: Allowing the current UNHCR refugee camp situation to grow and fester for years can only produce more radicalization and terrorism. A more expansive refugee policy with adequate security checks that resettles large numbers in safe countries can drain the swamp of potential future terrorists and decrease that risk.

## Where the Refugees Are Settling in the United States

The pace of Syrian refugee admissions is scheduled to pick up in 2016 unless Congress prevents it. In October 2015, the government took in 187 Syrian refugees and settled them in several states (Figures 1 and 2).

In October 2015, Syrians were approximately 3.6 percent of all refugees admitted, and many states didn't even receive any (Figure 3).

From the beginning of the Syrian civil war in 2011 through the first month of the 2016 fiscal year, a mere 0.63 percent of all refugees admitted to the United States were Syrians, or about 2,070 out of 329,856 (Figure 4).

## Conclusion

The security threat posed by refugees in the United States is insignificant. Halting America's processing of refugees due to a terrorist attack in another country that may have had one asylum-seeker as a co-plotter would be an extremely expensive overreaction to very minor threat. Resettling refugees who pass a thorough security check would likely decrease the recruiting pool for future terrorists and decrease the long-run risk.

The current refugee vetting system is multilayered, dynamic, and extremely effective. ISIS fighters or terrorists who are intent on attacking U.S. soil have myriad other options for doing so that are all cheaper, easier, and more likely to succeed than sneaking in through the heavily guarded refugee gate. The low level of current risk does not justify the government slamming that gate shut.

## Figure 1: Syrian Refugees Resettled in October 2015 by State

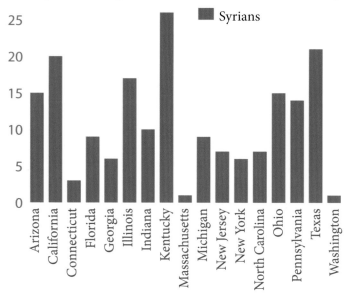

SOURCE: U.S. Refugee Processing Center.

## Figure 2: Other Refugees Resettled in States with Syrians October 2015

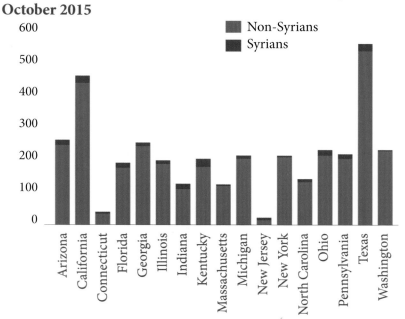

SOURCE: U.S. Refugee Processing Center.

## Figure 3: Syrian and Other Refugees by State

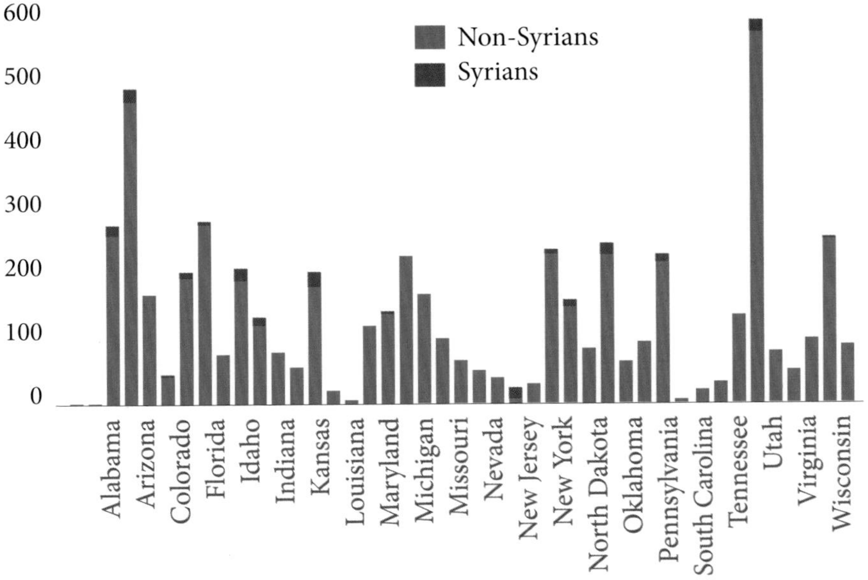

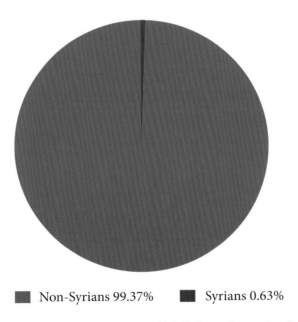

SOURCE: U.S. Refugee Processing Center.

## Figure 4: Syrian and Other Refugees Admitted Since 2011

Non-Syrians 99.37%     Syrians 0.63%

SOURCES: U.S. Department of State and U.S. Refugee Processing Center.

> *"Donald Trump's noisy complaints that immigration is out of control are literally true."*

# The Political Elite Don't Consider the Threats of Uncontrolled Immigration

*David Frum*

*In the following viewpoint, David Frum argues that there is a risk to uncontrolled immigration and that to deny this is to be willingly ignorant. He brings up highly publicized cases of immigrants who have carried out terrorist plots in the United States, including in San Bernardino in 2015. According to Frum, the data is undeniable: unrestricted immigration would pose a serious security and economic risk to the United States. David Frum is a senior editor at the* Atlantic *and the chairman of Policy Exchange. From 2001 to 2002, he was a speechwriter for President George W. Bush.*

As you read, consider the following questions:

1. Why does Frum suggest that the "political elites" are more likely to ignore the threat that uncontrolled immigration poses?
2. What data does Frum incorporate about Somali immigrants in the United States? Is this data convincing or not?
3. How are immigrants to the US dividing into "two streams"?

On Wednesday, FBI director James Comey alleged that the San Bernardino shooters were already plotting a mass-murder attack on the United States before Tafsheen Malik received the K-1 visa admitting her to the United States. Her husband-to-be, Syed Farook, was born a U.S. citizen. Yet his family's immigration history should also raise searching questions about the process by which would-be Americans are selected.

> Mr. Farook's father was an alcoholic and could be violent, capable of lashing out at his wife and children, according to statements his mother, Rafia Farook, made in a series of divorce proceedings beginning in 2006. The father, also named Syed Farook, called his wife names, screamed at his children, hurled home appliances and, at the worst moments, grew so combative that his children had to step between him and his wife, she asserted.
>
> The elder Mr. Farook forced his family to move out of their home in 2006, Ms. Farook said in court papers, but he continued to harass her. "My husband is mentally ill and is on medication but is also an alcoholic and drinks with the medicine," she said. The marriage was formally dissolved this year...
>
> A neighbor, Victor Venegas, said that the elder Mr. Farook had worked for him driving trucks until 2003 and would come around looking for money. "He would sometimes come over without calling," Mr. Venegas said, and ask, "Can I have $10 to buy cigarettes?"

It's not clear who exactly provided the first link in the chain of migration that brought the Farook clan to California and ultimately enabled the entry of Tashfeen Malik from Pakistan. That same chain, incidentally, also enabled the migration of Syed Farook's brother, also named Syed, who volunteered for the U.S. Navy shortly after 9/11 and served aboard the *USS Enterprise.*

However one assesses that chain and its consequences, it seems clear that the large majority of legal immigrants choose to come—or, more exactly, are chosen by their relatives—for their own reasons. They are not selected by the United States to advance some national interest. Illegal immigrants are of course entirely self-selected, as are asylum seekers. Even the refugee process, reportedly the most tightly screened, operates to a considerable extent outside national control: The first assessment of refugees is typically made by the UN High Commission on Refugees from within camps it operates. That explains why, for example, Christian Syrians make up only about 3 percent of the refugees admitted to the United States, despite accounting for 10 percent of the country's population: Fearing violence from Sunni Muslims, they apparently hesitate to enter UN camps in the first place.

Donald Trump's noisy complaints that immigration is out of control are literally true. Nobody is making conscious decisions about who is wanted and who is not, about how much immigration to accept and what kind to prioritize—not even for the portion of U.S. migration conducted according to law, much less for the larger portion that is not.

Nor is there much understanding of what has happened after it has happened. A simple question like, "How many immigrants are in prison?" turns out to be extraordinarily hard to answer. Poor information invites excessive fears, which are then answered with false assurances and angry accusations.

Nervous about Syrian refugees in the wake of the Paris massacre? How dare you! Would you turn away Jews fleeing Hitler? Oh, you think that analogy is hyperbolic? Tell it to the mayor of New York City.

This frequent invocation of the refugee trauma of the 1930s shuts down all discussion of anything that has happened since. Since 1991, the United States has accepted more than 100,000 Somali refugees. Britain accepted 100,000 as well. Some 50,000 Somali refugees were resettled in Canada; some 40,000 in Sweden; smaller communities were settled in the Netherlands, Norway, and Denmark.

How's that going?

- Minnesota is home to America's largest Somali community, 33,000 people. The unemployment rate for Somali Minnesotans in 2015 was triple the state average, 21 percent. As of 2014, about 5,950 of the state's Somali population received cash assistance; 17,000 receive food assistance as of 2014.
- A close study of Somali refugees by the government of Maine (home to the nation's second-largest Somali community) found that fewer than half of the working-age population had worked at any time in the five years from 2001 through 2006.
- The U.S. unemployment rate of 20+ percent still represents a huge improvement over rates in Europe. Only about 40 percent of working-age Somali men in Norway are employed. In the Swedish city of Malmo, home to one of the largest Somali communities in Europe, only 20 percent work.
- Somalis have so much difficulty finding work in the developed world because their skills badly mismatch local labor needs. Only about 18 percent of boys and 15 percent of girls attend even primary school in Somalia. UNICEF has given up trying to measure literacy rates. Much of the U.S. refugee population is descended from people held as slaves in Somalia, who accordingly lack any family tradition of education. Their children then flounder in Western schools, baffled by the norms and expectations they encounter there. In the U.K., Somali students pass the standard age 16 high school exams at a rate less than half that of Nigerian immigrant students.

- Struggling with the transition from semi-nomadic-herder society to postindustrial urban life, young Somalis in the West are tempted by criminal activity. Danish Somalis are 10 times more likely to be committed of a serious offense than native-born Danes. At least 29 young Canadian Somalis were murdered in drug-trafficking-related deaths between 2005 and 2010. In July 2012, Richard Stanek, sheriff of the county that encompasses Minneapolis-St. Paul, testified to Congress about the rising danger of American Somali gangs. While stressing that most Somalis in Minnesota obeyed the law, Stanek worried:

> Somali gangs have emerged as a serious threat to community safety both in Hennepin County and as a unique challenge to our law enforcement re- sources. These gangs are involved in multiple criminal activities that require sophisticated and resource-intensive law enforcement investigations. They are growing in influence and violence … and practice certain cultural behaviors that render some traditional U.S. criminal justice tools less effective.

- Other young Somalis turn to political and religious violence. An estimated 50 American Somalis returned to fight for al Shabab, committing some of the most heinous acts of that insurgency. One carried out a suicide bombing that killed 24 people in 2009. Al Shabab claimed three American Somalis took part in the attack on Nairobi's Westgate shopping mall in 2013 that killed at least 67 people. Al Shabab is now intensely recruiting American Somalis to undertake terror missions inside the United States.

> We call upon our Muslim brothers, particularly those in the West... imagine what a dedicated *mujahid* (fighter) in the West could do to the American and Jewish-owned shopping centers across the world.

What if such an attack was to call in the Mall of America in Minnesota, or the West Edmonton Mall in Canada? Or in London's Oxford Street, or any of the hundred or so Jewish-owned Westfield shopping centers dotted right across the Western world...

A growing number of Somali Americans in Minnesota have been charged with plotting to aid ISIS over the past two years, the 10th of them on December 9.

Immigration advocates understandably prefer to focus on the contributions of the refugees from Nazism than on less successful and more recent experiences.

Yet surely it is the more recent experiences that are more relevant. Pre-civil war Syria was no Somalia, but it was very far from a developed country. In 2010, the average Syrian had less than six years of schooling, less even than Egypt, according to the UN Development Index. Women were systematically subordinated: Only a quarter of Syrian women completed secondary education; only 13 percent participated in the workforce. Few Syrians will arrive with the skills of a modern economy, even apart from the language gap. Before the civil war, almost one-fifth of Syrians worked as agricultural laborers; about one-third worked in Syria's notoriously inefficient public sector.

How will these new arrivals adjust to the very different job markets of Western Europe and North America?

The European environment will prove especially challenging. Totaling benefits, mandated vacations, and so on, employers in the German private sector paid an average of 31.80 euros per hour per worker. And Germany—as expensive as it is—is actually one of the cheaper places to do business in Europe. The average French private sector employee costs 35.20 euros, the average Dane in the private sector, 42.0 euros. The cost of labor explains why such familiar American jobs as parking lot attendants, food runners in restaurants, and so on seem hardly to exist in northern Europe. It also explains why workers who cannot generate more than 31.80 euros in value for a business languish in protracted unemployment.

Germany in particular has tried to cope with this challenge by aggressively promoting low-wage work for the benefit of workers in the former East Germany and new immigrants. Some categories of work are exempted from standard benefit packages and minimum wage laws. But if first-generation migrants willingly accept this bargain, their children likely won't. Unfortunately, while a new population's expectations will rise in one generation, the accumulation of sufficient human capital to fulfill those expectations takes significantly longer. The predictable result: protracted underemployment across visibly identifiable subgroups of the population—group perceptions of inequity and injustice—resentment, radicalization, and criminal and political violence: the second-generation European Muslim experience in one grim economic equation.

For better or worse, producing low-wage jobs is one thing the U.S. economy can do in abundance. Where Americans have more difficulty is offering a path to upward mobility, especially for people born into the poorest one-fifth of the population. Not all migrants inhabit that bottom one-fifth. But disconcertingly many do—and contra the American Ellis Island myth, their children then stick there. America's poor immigrants don't usually arrive as refugees, of course. That distinction acquires great urgency in polemic. It has little meaning in real life.

If a refugee is someone "pushed" from his or her native land, and an immigrant is one "pulled" to a new country, then the vast majority of the tens of millions of people seeking to move from the poor global South to the rich North belong to both categories.

The tens of thousands of youthful border-crossers who claimed asylum in the United States in the summer of 2014 were described by supporters as refugees from gang violence at home in Central America. Yet 2014 was a year in which gang violence dramatically abated in Honduras and Guatemala. The "push" was

stronger two years earlier ... but the surge responded to the "pull"
of perceived opportunity.

Even with the Syrian refugees, "pull" matters as much as
"push." Most of the Syrians en route to Europe are immediately
fleeing—not the dictator Assad's barrel bombs—but the tedium
and futility of Turkish refugee camps. When European border
controls collapsed in the fall of 2015, Syrians and those claiming
to be Syrian rushed, not to any European country at random,
but very specifically to the countries with the strongest job
opportunities and most generous welfare systems: Germany and
Scandinavia. Every day, at the entrance to the Channel Tunnel,
young men described as "refugees" risk their lives to reach Britain
from ... France.

The distinction between migration and asylum-seeking is
grounded less in differences of motive, and more in an artifact
of international law. Shamed by the exclusion of German and
Austrian Jews in the 1930s, the post-World War II democracies
signed treaties and conventions that conferred rights of asylum
on persecuted people. If a person who wishes to resettle in one
country can gain recognition as an asylum-seeker, he cannot easily
be removed. Virtually all of the 51,000 Central Americans who
jumped the border in 2014 still remain in the United States. The
tens of thousands of Mediterranean crossers who falsely claimed
to be refugees when they disembarked in Italy likewise mostly
remain in Europe.

The immigration debate is defined by legal categories: migrant
versus refugee; illegal versus legal. Those legal categories are
subordinated, however, to a central political division: migrants
who are chosen by the receiving country versus those who choose
themselves. That political division in turn is connected to a fateful
economic division: migrants who arrive with the skills and attitudes
necessary to success in a modern advanced economy versus those
who don't.

Those divides are highlighted by a massive new study by
the National Academy of Sciences of the acculturation of new

# Problems in Europe

Frank-Jurgen Weise, head of the German Federal Office for Migration and Refugees (BAMF) took over leadership of the agency which has been in a constant state of disarray since the migrant crisis began last summer. The policy of the Merkel government has been to put pressure on the agency to get as many asylum seekers processed in the shortest amount of time.

Yet the priority of haste over thoroughness is starting to worry BAMF and Federal security agencies who consider the approach extremely dangerous in the wake of both the terrorist attacks in Paris, and the mass sexual assault in Cologne on New Years Eve.

Weise has decided that there needs to be more security checks of migrants and those coming to Germany to seek asylum. He notes the fact that perpetrators of both the Paris attacks and other arrests, such as the ISIS commander who was captured in a migrant home prove that radical Islamic terrorism is a present danger lurking in the mass flow of migrants coming into the European Union.

[...]

So far the speed at which the workers are able to process migrants has been less than hoped-for by the government. In 2016 so far, most staff at the agency process around 0.6 migrant hearings per day. The internal documents say that these numbers are "far below the expected values" and that the numbers the Merkel government would like to see would be at least seven times that which they are currently achieving.

[...]

Christian Democratic Union politician Wolfgang Bosbach said, "I can understand that the BAMF is proceeding under enormous pressure given the high numbers, But this should not compromise the security interests of the Federal Republic. In each case, nationality and identity as well as potential security-related information about an applicant must be clarified."

**"Concern That Fast Migrant Background Checks Are Letting Terrorists Into Europe Undetected," by Chris Tomlinson, Breitbart, March 8, 2016.**

immigrants to the United States: "The Integration of Immigrants into American Society." The first reports on the study in October headlined comforting news: recent immigrants to the United States were assimilating rapidly—arguably more rapidly than their predecessors of the pre-1913 Great Migration. One must read deeper into the report to encounter the worrying question: Assimilate to what? Like the country receiving them, immigrants to the United States are cleaved by class. Approximately one quarter of immigrants arrive with high formal educational qualifications: a college degree or more. Their record and that of their children is one of outstanding assimilation to the new American meritocratic elite, in many ways outperforming the native-born. (The highest outcomes are recorded for immigrants from India: 83 percent of male immigrants from India arrive with a college degree or higher.) College-educated immigrants are more likely to be employed than natives, and their children are more likely to complete a college degree in their turn. Here is a mighty contribution to the future wealth and power of the United States.

By contrast, about one-third of immigrants arrive with less than a high-school education. Immigrants from Latin America— the largest single group—arrive with the least education: Only about 13 percent of them have a college degree or more. They too assimilate to American life, but to the increasingly disorderly life of the American non-elite. Their children make educational progress as compared to the parents, but—worryingly—educational progress then stagnates or retrogresses in the third generation. For many decades to come, Latino families educationally lag well behind their non-Latino counterparts. The static snapshot is even more alarming: While 60 percent of Asian Americans over age 25 have at least a two-year diploma, as do 42 percent of non-Latino whites and 31 percent of African Americans, only 22 percent of Latino Americans do.

Partly as a result, as David Card and Stephen Raphael observe in their 2013 book on immigration and poverty, even third-generation Hispanic Americans are twice as likely to be poor as non-Latino whites.

When children of immigrants grow up poor, they assimilate to the culture of poorer America. While Mexicans in Mexico are slightly less likely to be obese than Americans, U.S. Latinos are considerably more likely to be obese than their non-Latino counterparts. The disparity is starkest among children: While 28 percent of whites under 19 are obese or overweight, 38 percent of Latino children are. American-born Latinos likewise are more likely to have children outside marriage than foreign-born Latinos.

This downward assimilation has stark real-world consequences. U.S.-born Latinos score lower on standardized tests and are more likely to drop out of high school than their non-Latino white counterparts. While those Latinos who do complete high school are slightly more likely than non-Latino whites to begin college, they are less likely to finish. Starting school without finishing burdens young people with the worst of all educational outcomes: college debt without a college degree.

About half of all immigrant-headed households accept some form of means-tested social welfare program. Those immigrant groups that arrive with the most education are, unsurprisingly, the least likely to require government assistance; those with the least require the most. Only 17 percent of households headed by an Indian immigrant use a means-tested program; 73 percent of households headed by a Central American immigrant do. (It's important to look at whole households because while undocumented immigrants who head a household may not be eligible for many means-tested programs, their U.S.-born children are.)

While Mexican immigrants are less likely to be sent to prison than the native-born, U.S.-born Hispanics are incarcerated at rates 50 percent higher than their parents and grandparents—and almost double that of U.S.-born whites.

In other words, immigrants to the United States are dividing into two streams. One arrives educated and assimilates "up"; the other, larger stream, arrives poorly educated and unskilled and assimilates "down." It almost ceases to make sense to speak and think of immigration as one product of one policy. Without ever having considered the matter formally or seriously, the U.S. has arrived at two different policies to serve two different sets of interests—and to achieve two radically different results, one very beneficial to U.S. society; the other, fraught with huge present and future social difficulties.

How did this happen? Almost perfectly unintentionally, suggests Margaret Sands Orchowski in her new history, *The Law That Changed the Face of America.* The Immigration Act of 1965 did two things, one well understood, one not: It abolished national quotas that effectively disfavored non-European immigration—and it established family reunification as the supreme consideration of U.S. immigration law. That second element has surprisingly proven even more important than the first. A migrant could arrive illegally, regularize his status somewhere along the way—for example, by the immigration amnesty of 1986—and then call his family from home into the United States after him. The 1965 act widened the flow of post-1970 low-skilled illegal immigration into a secondary and tertiary surge of further rounds of low-skilled immigration that continues to this day.

Americans talk a lot about the social difficulties caused by large-scale, low-skill immigration, but usually in a very elliptical way. Giant foundations—Pew, Ford—spend lavishly to study the problems of the new low-skill immigrant communities. Public policy desperately seeks to respond to the challenges presented by large-scale low-skill immigration. But the fundamental question— "should we be doing this at all?"—goes unvoiced by anyone in a position of responsibility. Even as the evidence accumulates that the policy was a terrible mistake from the point of view of the pre-existing American population, elites insist that the policy is unquestionable ... more than unquestionable, that the only possible revision of the policy is to accelerate future flows of low-skill immigration even faster, whether as migrants or as refugees or in some other way.

Even as immigration becomes ever-more controversial with the larger American public, within the policy elite it preserves an unquestioned status as something utterly beyond discussion. To suggest anything otherwise is to suggest—not merely something offensive or objectionable—but something self-evidently impossible, like adopting cowrie shells as currency or Donald Trump running for president.

Only Donald Trump is running for president—and doing pretty well, too. He's led polls of Republican presidential candidates for now nearly 5 consecutive months. Pundits (including me!) who had insisted that it was impossible that he could actually win the nomination are now beginning to ponder what will happen if he somehow does. And while it's clear that the immigration issue does not constitute all of Trump's appeal, it's equally clear that the issue has been indispensable to that appeal.

Until this very year, Trump's few sparse comments on immigration fell neatly within the elite consensus. In a December 2012 Newsmax interview, Trump blamed Mitt Romney's recent presidential defeat on Romney's "self-deportation" comments. Trump endorsed the then conventional that the GOP's immigration message had been "mean-spirited" in 2012 and invite more people to become "wonderful, productive citizens of this country."

What seems to have changed Trump's mind is a book: *Adios America* by Ann Coulter. The phrase "political book of the year" is a usually an empty compliment, but if the phrase ever described any book, *Adios America* is it. In its pages, Trump found the message that would convulse the Republican primary and upend the dynastic hopes of former-frontrunner Jeb Bush. Perhaps no single writer has had such immediate impact on a presidential election since Harriet Beecher Stowe.

*Adios America* is an avalanche of an essay, a cascading torrent of quips, facts, and statistics. Furiously polemical, mercilessly indignant, utterly indifferent to balance and context, Coulter batters the reader with what might be called the "reverse valedictorian": instead of the usual heartwarming stories of immigrant success, she immerses the reader in incidents of immigrant crime, failure, and welfare abuse.

> A Chinese immigrant in New York, Dong Lu Chen, bludgeoned his wife to death with a claw hammer because she was having an affair. He was unashamed, greeting his teenaged boy at the door in bloody clothes, telling the boy he had just killed mom. Brooklyn Supreme Court Justice Edward Pincus let Chen off with probation—for murder—after an anthropologist testified that, in Chinese culture, the shame of a man being cuckolded justified murder ... The female head of the Asian-American Defense and Education Fund, Margaret Fung, applauded Chen's light sentence, saying that harsher penalty would "promote the idea that when people come to America they have to give up their way of doing things. That is an idea we cannot support." At least Chen came to the United States based on his specialized knowledge of nuclear cell extraction biology. No, I'm sorry—Chen emigrated to the United States with his entire family when he was fifty years old—fifteen years away from collecting Social Security—to be a dishwasher.
>
> Two of the most famous murder sprees of the 1990s were also perpetrated by legal immigrants. The 1993 Long Island Railroad massacre that left six passengers dead was committed by Jamaican-immigrant Colin Ferguson ... In 1997, Christopher Burmeister, a twenty-seven year old musician, was shot in the head and killed by Palestinian immigrant Ali Hassan Abu Kamal at the top of the Empire State Building. Burmeister's band mate, Matthew Gross, also took a bullet to the head but—after eight hours of surgery—survived. Gross now lives in a group home in Montclair, New Jersey, with other brain-damaged men, taking daily medication for his seizures. The assailant, Abu Kamal, had immigrated to America with his entire family two month earlier—at age sixty-eight. It's a smart move to bring in older immigrants well past their productive years, so we can start paying out Social Security right away.

Coulter's core message, "immigration isn't working as promised," is joined to a second message equally central to the Donald Trump campaign: "We are governed by idiots."

Those are messages that resonate only louder after the San Bernardino massacre, in which one of the killers entered the country on a fiancée visa issued to a nonexistent address in Pakistan.

But the truth is actually far scarier: No, America is not governed by idiots. It's governed mostly by capable and conscientious people who are simply overwhelmed by the scale of the immigration challenge. The UN High Commission on Refugees estimates that 60 million people have been displaced by war or natural disaster. Millions of them would wish to move to Europe or North America if they could. That population will only grow in the years ahead: Nigeria, a country of an estimated 137 million people today, is projected to reach 400 million within the next 35 years, overtaking the United States. How many of them will wish to leave behind their failed state for opportunities in the global North? Even in Mexico, a middle-income country by global standards, more than half of young people in their 20s would like to move to the United States if they could.

One reason we hear so much about the Jewish refugees of the 1930s, to circle back to where I started, is the natural human tendency to wish away overwhelming problems. If the word "refugee" conjures up Albert Einstein, Kurt Weill, Hans Bethe, Lawrence Tribe, Billy Wilder, and Henry Kissinger—well, what country wouldn't welcome as many as it could get?

But that's not the story of Syria. Syria is embroiled in a civil war with hundreds of thousands of combatants. Most of the killing has been done by the army of President Bashar al-Assad and now, his Iranian and Russian allies. President Obama said at his November 16 press conference in Antalya, Turkey, "We also have to remember that many of these refugees are the victims of terrorism themselves—that's what they're fleeing." Many of his hearers mentally amended the president's words to a claim that the Syrian refugees are fleeing the terrorism of ISIS. But this president always speaks carefully, and that's not what he said, even if he didn't mind being misheard. Interviews with the refugees themselves confirm that most are fleeing the violence perpetrated by the Assad

regime, not the deranged fanaticism of ISIS. While comparatively
few Syrians—or Muslims anywhere—have any sympathy for ISIS
ideology, the majority of Syrians espouse some form of Sunni
fundamentalist religious belief, a fundamentalism that Western
societies asked to open their doors are entitled to find disquieting.

Also disquieting is the way in which refugee advocates toggle
back and forth between reassuring the West that there is nothing
to fear—and warning of terrorist violence if the refugees are
refused. Here's Michael Ignatieff, a noted writer on refugee issues
and former leader of the Liberal Party of Canada in *The New York
Times* in September:

> What must Syrians, camped on the street outside the Budapest
> railway station, be thinking of all that fine rhetoric of ours about
> human rights and refugee protection? If we fail, once again, to
> show that we mean what we say, we will be creating a generation
> with abiding hatred in its heart.

Ignatieff is right to express concern about the hatred sweeping
the Middle East. But to many Americans—and Canadians too, and
Europeans, and other Westerners—it may seem reckless to respond
to that hatred by inviting more of it into their own countries,
and more reckless than ever after the Paris and San Bernardino
jihadist atrocities. Obama and much of the elite media find that
reaction cowardly, contemptible and even "shameful"—his word.
But in a democracy, leaders who dismiss and denigrate widespread
concerns soon find themselves ex-leaders. Everywhere in the
Western world there is a fast-growing constituency for new kinds of
immigration and refugee policies. If anything is shameful, it is the
shabby, thoughtless, and arrogant elite consensus that has to date
denied that constituency a responsible political leadership. But that
too is changing, yielding to heavy evidence and hard experience.

> *"Syrian refugees are generally afraid*
> *of exactly the same thing that*
> *Americans are: Islamist terrorism."*

# Few Facts Are Used in the Debate over Resettling Refugees in the United States

*Lauren Gambino, Patrick Kingsley,*
*and Alberto Nardelli*

*In the following viewpoint, Lauren Gambino, Patrick Kingsley, and Alberto Nardelli examine what is true and false in the morass of political discourse involving Syrian refugees and their resettlement in the United States. Provoked by the Syrian civil war from 2011 until the present day, a refugee crisis has encompassed the globe and is one of the worst such crises since World War II. Many American politicians, particularly ideologically conservative governors, have stated their intent not to allow any Syrian refugees on American soil or at least in their states. But the fear over Syrian refugees, according to these authors, is largely based on misconceptions and falsehoods. Gambino is a reporter in New York for the* Guardian, *Kingsley is the paper's migration correspondent, and Nardelli is its data editor.*

As you read, consider the following questions:

1. Why have politicians in the United States objected to resettling Syrian refugees, including children under the age of five?
2. What is the kind of vetting process that Syrian refugees must go through in order to enter the United States?
3. Why are Syrian refugees unlikely to be Islamic State, or ISIS, supporters?

Congressional Republicans voted on Thursday to make it more difficult for refugees from Syria and Iraq to come to the US as the fallout from last Friday's Isis terrorist attacks in Paris continues.

In addition, more than half of the US's governors have said they will no longer provide placement for Syrian refugees, arguing that they pose too great a risk to national security.

New Jersey governor and Republican presidential candidate Chris Christie has said his state will not take in any refugees—"not even orphans under the age of five."

Louisiana governor Bobby Jindal has said he has directed state police to "track" the Syrian refugees in his state, something his state police have played down.

GOP presidential hopefuls Ted Cruz and Jeb Bush have suggested the US government prioritize Christian refugees.

Barack Obama has pledged to veto the legislation, and has condemned the anti-refugee comments as "un-American," but experts worry the backlash could have dangerous consequences if these claims go unchecked.

"Sowing fear of refugees is exactly the kind of response groups like Isis are seeking," said Iain Levine, deputy executive director for program at Human Rights Watch, on Thursday. "Yes, governments need to bring order to refugee processing and weed out militant extremists, but now more than ever they also need to stand with people uprooted from their homes by ideologies of hatred and help them find real protection."

Here we try to separate fact from fiction in the US debate over Syrian refugees.

## Could dangerous refugees come to the US and carry out a Paris-style attack?

The American backlash against refugees is based largely on the fear that a Paris-style attack could be replicated in America if the US began to shoulder its burden of the refugee crisis.

But such a fear is misguided because the process of relocating refugees to America is very different from the way that refugees currently arrive in Europe. Syrians flown to the US will be the most heavily vetted group of people currently allowed into the US, according to the State Department.

Each candidate is vetted first by the UN's refugee agency, and then separately by officials from the State Department, the FBI, the Department of Homeland Security and the Defense Department. The process takes between 18 months and two years.

By contrast, a refugee hoping to reach Europe can pay a smuggler approximately $1,000 (£660) to take them in a dinghy across the six-mile-wide strait between Turkey and the Greek islands.

Upon arrival, a refugee is fingerprinted and then allowed to reach the European mainland even if they do not have identification documents. They are then transported through a succession of European countries until they reach more welcoming countries, such as Germany, Austria and Sweden, where many of them claim asylum. Due to Europe's Schengen system, which allows anyone to pass between most of the countries in the EU without having to show their passport, a migrant could then easily reach Paris without ever being given a background check by any government official.

## European Union (EU) Emergency Relocation

ARRIVALS TO ITALY AND GREECE BY SEA IN 2015: 817,416

NUMBER OF REFUGEES EU MEMBER STATES HAVE
PLEDGED TO RELOCATE FROM GREECE AND ITALY:
160,000

PLACES MADE AVAILABLE SO FAR: 3,216 OF 160,000

PEOPLE RELOCATED SO FAR: 158 OF 160,000

SOURCE: European Commission, UNHCR

## Is the US taking in large numbers of Syrian refugees?

Despite fears that an influx of Syrian refugees would overrun the country, so far, the US has welcomed just a fraction of the millions of refugees who have fled Syria. Since 2012, the US has accepted 2,174 Syrian refugees—roughly 0.0007% of America's total population.

The refugees the US takes in are among the most vulnerable in the Syrian conflict: many are women and their children, while others are religious minorities and victims of violence or torture.

Obama has committed to taking 10,000 Syrian refugees in the coming year, five times the number the US has taken in the past four years. Were the country to take in an additional 10,000 Syrians, they would still only represent approximately 0.004% of its existing population. This ratio stands in marked contrast with the much poorer and much smaller countries bearing the biggest burden of the Syrian refugee crisis.

Lebanon, whose population was previously an estimated 4.5 million, now has a Syrian refugee population of roughly 1.2 million—meaning that around one in five Lebanese residents is a Syrian refugee. Turkey, which houses more Syrian refugees than any other country, has welcomed 2 million, or 2.67% of its total population of 75 million.

EU member states agreed in September to relocate 160,000 people in "clear need of international protection" through a scheme set up to relocate Syrian, Eritrean and Iraqi refugees from the most affected EU states—such as Greece and Italy—to others.

So far only 158 refugees have been relocated. However, the relocation scheme is only one facet of how Europe is dealing with the wider refugee crisis. Some 880,000 asylum applications have been lodged across the EU's 28 member states so far this year, compared with 625,920 in all of 2014 and 431,090 in 2013. This year's figures have been the highest on record.

More than 230,000 Syrians have applied for asylum across the EU this year, and nearly 45% of these applications have been lodged in Germany alone.

Nearly 80,000 Syrians have been granted asylum in the EU so far this year. But the figure for migrants granted asylum does not reveal the full scale of the number of people that some European countries are welcoming. Filing and processing paperwork takes time.

For example, between January and October, Germany registered the arrival of 243,721 asylum seekers from Syria. The country expects to receive more than a million asylum seekers this year.

Canada resettled 3,089 Syrian refugees between 1 January 2014 and 3 November 2015. However, recently elected prime minister Justin Trudeau has committed to resettling 25,000 Syrians by the end of the year.

## Countries Granting Asylum to Syrian Refugees, 2015

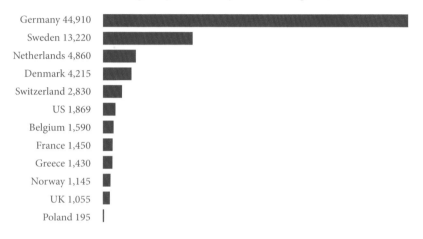

SOURCE: Eurostat, Refugee Processing Center

## Refugees and Population
NUMBER OF SYRIAN REFUGEES PER 1,000 PEOPLE

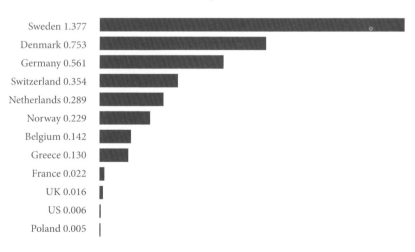

SOURCE: Eurostat, Refugee Processing Center

## Are Syrian refugees likely to be Isis sympathizers?

Syrian refugees are generally afraid of exactly the same thing that Americans are: Islamist terrorism. Many are fleeing areas held by the Islamic State, and they are doing so in contravention of Isis edicts. On a dozen occasions, Isis has condemned refugees for fleeing Isis areas.

"For those who want to blame the attacks on Paris on refugees, you might want to get your facts straight," wrote Aaron Zelin, an analyst of jihadis, in a blogpost. "The reality is, [Isis] loathes that individuals are fleeing Syria for Europe. It undermines [Isis's] message that its self-styled Caliphate is a refuge."

By rejecting Syrian refugees, American governors are in fact helping Isis, because they are proving Isis's argument that the west does not want to assist Syrian Muslims, and that their only salvation lies in Isis.

"Syrian and Iraqi refugees are the victims of terrorism, fleeing the same type of atrocities that we've recently witnessed," said Shelly Pitterman, of the United Nations Office of the High Commissioner for Refugees (UNHCR) on Wednesday. "They've rejected the ideology of extremism and share the values of freedom and tolerance."

### Refugee Resettlement, United States

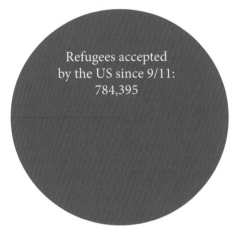

Number of those accepted who have been arrested on terrorism charges: 3

Refugees accepted by the US since 9/11: 784,395

SOURCE: State Department, Migration Policy Institute

## Are governors able to ban Syrian refugees?

More than half of the US's governors have said they will not relocate refugees in their state, even though it is not within their power to do so. The US government has sole authority over whether immigrants and refugees of any nationality enter the US.

Yet because of the way the government works with states to resettle refugees, there are actions states could take to disrupt the process. States can wield the power they do have to block funding from funneling through to programs that serve refugees, such as English language classes and job training programs designed to help them integrate into society.

"There is some soft power being exerted by the states here even if there's not hard legal ground for the state to stand on," said Pratheepan Gulasekaram, an associate professor of law at Santa Clara University. "If this becomes a trend, I think it sets an extremely dangerous precedent."

To distinguish which refugees will or will not be resettled based on their religion or national origin raises constitutional and legal problems, Gulasekaram said, adding: "States can't pick and choose amongst refugees."

"Accepting refugees into the United States is one of our grandest traditions. And we've been doing it since the beginning even before we were a nation," said Lee Williams, vice-president and chief financial officer of US Committee for Refugees and Immigrants, one of the nine nine national agencies that handle refugee resettlement in the US.

"It would be a real black mark on the United States's reputation were we to stop this process, though I hope we won't get to that point."

> *"Anyone who tells me Germany is full up, or that we can't afford them, I say think of our past, and of the future. Of course we can afford them—we're a rich country, and we have a duty to help those in need."*

# We Have a Duty to Help Those in Need

*Jason M. Breslow*

*In the following viewpoint, Jason M. Breslow uses a German town named Goslar as a case study for how different approaches to accepting refugees can work. In a country that has experienced several high-profile Islamic terrorist attacks in recent years, the mayor of this town is dedicated to proving that refugees do not pose a danger to Germans and that they provide opportunities instead. Perhaps more important, he believes, we have a moral obligation to help those in need. Breslow argues that for German towns like Goslar, some possible benefits can include raising the amount of people in an otherwise aging or stagnant population, which can have important economic benefits as well. Breslow is digital editor at* Frontline *and has worked as a reporter and producer for the* Boston Globe, PBS NewsHour, *and the* Chronicle of Higher Education.

"Welcome to Goslar, Where the Mayor Wants More Refugees," from the FRONTLINE website for "Children of Syria," (http://www.pbs.org/wgbh/frontline/article/welcome-to-goslar-where-the-mayor-wants-more-refugees) WGBH, 1995-2016 WGBH Educational Foundation.

As you read, consider the following questions:

1. Why is the town of Goslar's approach to immigrants different from that of other Germany towns?
2. What is the Königstein Key? What repercussions does it hold for immigrants who arrive in Germany?
3. Why might a country such as Germany be more interested in welcoming refugees than, for example, the United States?

When Farah, Helen, Mohammed and Sara arrived in the small German town of Goslar last year, what the four child refugees saw could not have been more different than the life they'd left behind in war-torn Syria.

"There isn't a single shelled house," their mother, Hala, noticed on their first drive into town. "It's safe and we won't be afraid anymore," said Helen. "When we first came here this morning, the birds were saying, 'Welcome to Germany' … I think they might be happy. They're happy we're here in Germany."

The family of five—who are featured in the below scene from the new FRONTLINE documentary, *Children of Syria*—is among the more than 1 million refugees to arrive in Germany in 2015. While the government of Chancellor Angela Merkel has repeatedly called on Germans to be more welcome, the stream of asylum seekers has nonetheless roiled the nation's politics.

In the first half of 2015, Germany witnessed 199 attacks on refugee hostels, and in recent months, protests against the nation's immigration policy have taken place in cities across the country, including Berlin, Dresden, Hamburg and Leipzig. Last month, backlash to Merkel's immigration stance propelled the anti-refugee Alternative for Germany party to big gains in regional elections.

But in Goslar, a picturesque town of just 50,000, Mayor Oliver Junk is trying to counter the anti-immigrant sentiment growing not just in Germany, but across much of Europe. With Goslar's population shrinking by around 2,000 people per year as young people flee to bigger cities and older residents die, Junk sees refugees as key to the town's future.

"Europeans must welcome and integrate refugees, accepting that they are not a burden but a great opportunity," Junk wrote in an op-ed published last month in the policy journal Europe's World. "We have to keep sight of the most essential issue: to support refugees is our most fundamental humanitarian duty."

Junk, a lawyer by training and a member of Merkel's Christian Democrats party, says refugees can revive Goslar's economy by moving into empty houses and applying for jobs that have gone unfilled. Schools have closed in Goslar, and in some parts of town, homes are either sitting empty or have been demolished.

In 2014, the broader district of Goslar, which as a region has approximately 135,000 residents, received about 400 refugees, according to Junk. Last year, the district took in around 1,900 new arrivals.

Before new arrivals move into their homes in Goslar, they spend six weeks living in what the city calls its integration center, where they receive language courses and lessons in German culture.

Refugees who are granted asylum are provided a monthly stipend by the German government, as well as other assistance. When Hala and her four children arrived in 2015, for example, they were given around $2,200 per month, a new home, free health care and education.

Despite Junk's enthusiasm for more refugees, reversing the decline in population has been a difficult climb.

German asylum policy is one factor. The challenge for towns like Goslar is a 1949 law known as the "Königsteiner Schlüssel," or Königstein Key. Designed to more fairly distribute the financial burden of taking in new refugees, the law requires Germany to relocate them within the country's 16 states based on population and tax base, as opposed to need or available space.

Refugees who are granted asylum are randomly relocated through an electronic system, meaning small towns like Goslar are only eligible to accept a few hundred refugees, while larger, wealthy cities are responsible for a larger share of the burden. Munich, for example, was assigned 15,000 in 2015.

But many larger cities have struggled to keep up with the pace of arrivals. Some have been forced to close shelters because of overcrowding. In Munich, authorities even considered placing refugees in one of the large tents left over from the Oktoberfest festival.

In big cities, "housing space is scarce," Junk told FRONTLINE by email. "In contrast, cities like Goslar have to struggle with a permanent decline in population. I used to say that refugees are a chance to oppose vacant flats and shortage of skilled workers. I still see this chance when a reasonable policy of integration is pursued."

Amid the growing anti-immigrant sentiment, however, changing the law in Germany may prove difficult. In the meantime, Junk is working to convince other small town mayors into adopting his position toward migrants, and has offered to take in refugees from nearby cities that are struggling to manage.

"They say to me, 'rules are rules.' It's typically rigid and German, always having to work with finished concepts rather than allowing for new ideas," Junk said last summer. "Anyone who tells me Germany is full up, or that we can't afford them, I say think of our past, and of the future. Of course we can afford them—we're a rich country, and we have a duty to help those in need."

| "*Biometric measures have tended to discriminate against migrants deliberately as part of a policy to tackle illegal immigration and as an unavoidable consequence of their contact with borders.*"

# Biometric Technology Is Discriminatory and Does Not Prevent Terrorism

*Rebekah Thomas*

*In the following viewpoint, the ways in which biometric technology, instituted since the terrorist attacks of September 11, 2001, are particularly discriminatory toward migrants. While the author admits that there are some important benefits to biometrics, she shows that biometrics have important weaknesses as well and can cause trauma for certain populations of immigrants. However, she asserts, there is a way to find "common ground" for both those concerned with security and immigrant rights. Thomas is associate policy and research officer at the Global Commission on International Migration in Geneva and a specialist in international human rights law.*

Originally published by the Migration Policy Institute as: Rebekah Thomas, "Biometrics, Migrants, and Human Rights," Migration Information Source, March 1, 2005. http://www.migrationpolicy.org/article/biometrics-migrants-and-human-rights.

As you read, consider the following questions:

1. What are biometrics and when were they
   largely implemented?
2. What are some weaknesses of biometrics?
3. Why might biometrics be particularly discriminatory
   toward migrants and particularly immigrants from
   third-world countries?

In recent years, heightened security concerns arising from
the growth of transnational crime and terrorism have led
to increased interest and research into biometric technology's
potential to make accurate identity checks. Long used in the realm
of criminal proceedings, as well as in the private and commercial
sector, biometrics have received a great deal of attention as a way
of "filling the gaps" in traditional methods of border control.

Biometrics are physiological or behavioral characteristics used
to recognize or verify the identity of a living person. Physiological
characteristics include fingerprints, hand geometry, iris shape, face,
voice, ear shape, and body odor. Behavioral characteristics include
hand-written signatures and the way a person walks.

Any one of these types of biometric information can allow
border security guards to make rapid and precise, one-to-one
(authentication) or one-to-many (verification), identity checks.
In simple terms, a one-to-one check determines whether a person
is who he claims to be, such as when a signature is compared to one
on a legal document. A one-to-many check entails the identification
of one person from among many—for instance, when a fingerprint
is compared to thousands of fingerprints in a database.

Border checks in both the EU and USA have opted for
inkless fingerprints and digital facial recognition through
digitized photographs. Saudi Arabia has chosen to use iris
recognition technology.

The events of September 11, 2001, were the trigger for a flurry
of developments in the biometrics field. The USA Patriot Act,

passed in October 2001, introduced measures requiring all foreign visitors to provide machine-readable, biometric travel documents, and put into place an entry-exit system to monitor movements to and from the country. This legislation prompted a number of other countries to adapt their travel documents accordingly and to set up biometric identity checks to ensure border security.

However, there are important human rights implications inherent in the collection, processing, and distribution of a person's unique, physical identifiers, causing a certain degree of friction between the security interests of policymakers and the right to privacy of those subject to any of these measures. This friction is at the heart of the biometrics debate.

It is important to look at this debate from the migrants' perspective because the development of biometric technology is particularly discriminatory towards migrants, both in its application and its effect.

## Right to Privacy and Biometrics

Advocates suggest that biometrics should enhance rather than conflict with individual privacy, preventing identity theft and providing increased anonymity for the user. An automated identity check will simply verify that the codified data encrypted on a travel document corresponds to that provided at the border check. However, biometrics still potentially challenge the right of bodily and information privacy and the right to process and distribute this information.

Privacy is a fundamental human right upheld under Article 12 of the Universal Declaration of Human Rights, as well as Article 17 of the UN International Covenant on Civil and Political Rights and inasmuch applies to all people, regardless of nationality, immigration status, age, or sex.

Privacy is also defended at the regional level, both in Europe and the U.S., under their respective human rights conventions, and is equally applicable to all people residing within those jurisdictions. In addition, these rights are enforceable rights under the Inter-American Court, the European Commission, and the European Court of Human Rights. More specifically, the UN International Convention on the Protection of the Rights of All Migrant Workers and Their Families (ICMW), which entered into force in 2003 and has been ratified by 27 countries, provides both regular and irregular migrant workers with a right to privacy under Article 14.

The right to information privacy is assured through data protection mechanisms, which exist in one form or another across the world. The UN General Assembly has devised guidelines of "minimum guarantees" for the use of personal computerized data, as have the Council of Europe and the Organization for Economic Cooperation and Development (OECD). It is up to individual countries to incorporate these guidelines into national legislation protecting personal data.

All of the above instruments share four key principles. Firstly, data must be obtained lawfully. Second, it also must be kept safely and securely. Third, it must be accurate and up-to-date, and finally, it must only be used for the original purpose specified. In addition, data protection ideally includes some type of enforcement mechanism.

In practice, however, it can be difficult to uphold these principles. For example, one of the weaknesses of biometrics is their lack of reliability, whether from error or from their vulnerability to interference.

"Contactless" RFID (Radio Frequency Identification) chips, a favored tool among private consumer companies to track inventories of clothing and other consumer goods, can be read from a distance of up to 20 meters, enabling any non-official person equipped with a biometric reader to obtain this information anonymously. Furthermore, in the U.S., the stored information is not encrypted, and therefore more easily "read."

A second weakness of biometrics is that it is not always accurate. For example, the relative reliability of fingerprint checks is not only likely to decrease over time, but also as more data accumulates in giant databases.

Another weakness is "function creep," which means data is used in a way not foreseen nor consented to at the time the data was collected. The fallibility of RFID chips, coupled with the use of huge national or regional databases to store biometrics information, highlights the concerns linked to function creep.

However, function creep seems somewhat inevitable as national governments seek to enhance global interoperability between databases, which facilitate the exchange of data between national immigration, law enforcement, and other public and private databases, such as those used by airline and travel agencies.

The more this data is transferred across different agencies and countries, the greater the risk of it seeping into controversial areas of immigration control, such as tracking and surveillance. Such a scheme has already been adopted in Britain, where registered asylum seekers are monitored using biometric "tagging"—for instance, an anklet bracelet with global satellite positioning requiring the asylum seeker to be at home at certain times—as an alternative to detention.

Although these principles are important, they can only be effective if they are enforced. The European Union (EU) has recognized the need for enforcement by establishing a Data Protection Directive (95/46 EC, building on previous measures) to be incorporated into Member States' national laws. This directive is overseen by an independent working party comprised of national data commissioners of Member States. The working party's mandate is to ensure the uniform application of the directive's general principles.

The U.S., however, has perhaps the weakest laws in terms of data protection. Although the U.S. is a signatory to the OECD guidelines, it has not implemented them. Data protection laws have developed on an adhoc basis, with industry-specific codes of practice governed by a mix of legislation, regulation, and self-regulation, but no federal-level law or enforcement agency.

To facilitate commerce with the EU after the EU Data Protection Directive went into effect, the U.S. devised the "safe harbor" framework. This allows a non-regulated list of U.S. companies, which have put secure procedures in place for handling sensitive data, to comply with the directive.

Yet even where such mechanisms are in place, the question arises whether existing protection is appropriate and sufficient to cover all the uncharted territory that accompanies biometrics. The new EU Commissioner for Justice, Freedom and Security has stressed that safeguards "need to be maintained, respected, and reviewed in the light of the development of networks, technologies, and the types of data used, for example, in relation to the possibility of the extensive use of biometrics."

Furthermore, even should there exist sufficient safeguards governing one country or group of states, the exchange of this information across borders throws into question which and whose data protection rules should apply.

## Migrants and Biometrics

Biometric measures have tended to discriminate against migrants deliberately as part of a policy to tackle illegal immigration and as an unavoidable consequence of their contact with borders. Immigrants from third-world countries, for example, are more likely to need visas for entry into the U.S., and certain nationals and ethnic groups are deliberately targeted by immigration controls because of terrorism fears.

Many pilot projects have targeted narrow and specific groups. These include the UK's visa registration project, the early U.S. SEVIS program (Student and Exchange Visitor Information Program, an electronic system for maintaining information on international students and exchange visitors in the United States), and the U.S. NSEERS program (National Security Entry-Exit System). The UK project targeted visa applicants from five East African countries as well as asylum seekers, while the U.S. programs were aimed at foreign students and Arab-Muslim travelers, respectively.

Biometrics are also used at certain airports' border checkpoints as part of "frequent flyer" programs for business travelers and airline employees. These programs include CANPASS in Canadian airports, INSPASS in major U.S. airports, and PRIVIUM in Amsterdam's Schiphol airport; Italy and the UK have similar programs. However, such programs are considerably less controversial because they are based on the voluntary surrender of fingerprints, hand images, or digital photographs.

In addition to this deliberate discrimination, immigrants and asylum seekers wanting to cross borders may also suffer disproportionately from the negative effects of this technology. The very act of collecting biometric information and the implications of such a procedure—the stigma of criminal activity attached to fingerprints or "mugshots" for example, or even the hygiene-related issues of touching a finger scan—might be felt more acutely within different cultural groups.

For asylum seekers—generally people fleeing their country for fear of persecution who may have an acquired distrust of authority—such a procedure may not only be objectionable in principle, but may be a terrifying and traumatic experience.

Function creep also presents far greater problems for migrants, both temporary and permanent, insofar as biometrics may be incorporated into identity cards and multipurpose entitlement cards. The particular link between immigration and law enforcement bodies serves to further stimulate the perception of migrants as criminals, as well as to provide a pretext for identification-based stop and search procedures that tend to target ethnic minority communities.

In addition, public health bodies have already started warning against the exclusionary nature of entitlement cards that may exclude vulnerable people from essential medical treatment or discourage those without cards from seeking care.

## Arguments for and Against Biometrics

Biometrics advocates argue these effects are an unavoidable price to pay to ensure border security.

In the fight against illegal migration, biometric identifiers certainly present a number of advantages. They may facilitate return procedures of failed asylum seekers by identifying their true country of origin, as well as prevent multiple asylum claims and "visa shopping" (simultaneous applications), by keeping a centralized, easily accessible database.

Biometrics might even contribute to reducing discrimination, advocates say, by automating identity checks and raising confidence in border security and immigration controls, thereby reducing the myths and stereotypes associated with migrants and asylum seekers. With biometrics, asylum seekers would be able to provide credible, immutable evidence of their claim, and traffickers would be hindered in their attempts to use false identities.

Yet many of these measures would target nationals of particular countries who are entitled to the fundamental rights enshrined in international and regional human rights conventions. Applying these measures in such a discriminatory fashion would almost certainly violate their right to privacy.

Aside from discrimination, data protection principles are key to preventing the worst effects of biometrics. Some migrants suffer from social exclusion, perhaps as a result of linguistic and cultural barriers, or they may lack judicial remedy depending on national laws.

Weak or unclear data protection rules amplify the risk to migrants since they may be reluctant to affirm their rights or may be unfamiliar with the nature, extent, and operation of these rights. Given migrants' exposure to biometric systems that are now being critically reexamined for technical flaws, data protection and legal redress should assume an even greater role.

However, the importance of data protection has been blurred by a distorted emphasis on security and border controls that may compromise privacy rights. The effects are threefold.

First, the priority given to security issues may work against the need to protect and provide for migrants' rights given their particular vulnerability to such measures. Some contend that security concerns are in part a cover for a general reluctance to fulfil these obligations.

This prioritization reveals a widespread practice that considers even fundamental rights, such as privacy, as dependent on legal status or nationality. Such an interpretation is clearly contrary to the provisions of international law cited above, and overlooks the fact that even irregular migrants are entitled to human rights.

Second, the association of biometrics with anti-terrorism measures has linked biometrics procedures with terrorism. Consequently, although identity checks at borders are a recognized and accepted immigration procedure, the use of biometric information has contributed to the criminalization of this process.

Third, security issues seem to operate as a universal key that can open doors previously locked by data protection and privacy concerns. These measures are gaining social acceptance without proper consideration either of their long-term effects or of alternative methods.

So far, there is little evidence from the U.S. and UK that biometric technology has contributed to reducing either terrorism or irregular migration. According to the U.S. Department of Homeland Security, more than 200 persons have been arrested since the January 2004 launch of US-VISIT, a program that electronically tracks the entry and exit of foreign visitors using biographical information and biometric identifiers. Those arrested include "convicted rapists, drug traffickers, individuals convicted of credit card fraud, a convicted armed robber, and numerous immigration violators and individuals attempting visa fraud."

However, having processed over 2.5 million visitors, no terrorist suspects have been caught to date, and these statistics do nothing to change the numbers of migrants who enter legitimately, but who become irregular once inside the country.

Similarly, in the UK, a six-month biometrics visa trial in July 2003 targeted exclusively visitors from Sri Lanka; the trial uncovered seven undocumented migrants. Based on this "success," the UK announced plans to extend the project to include nationals from Djibouti, Eritrea, Ethiopia, Tanzania, and Uganda.

## The Future of Security and Human Rights

Nevertheless, security and human rights may not necessarily be incompatible principles, and the development of biometric technology can operate within a context that reconciles the needs and rights of all parties.

Finding that common ground requires reconsideration of three points.

First, the use of biometric documents must be proportional to the risk faced and the consequent restrictions placed on freedom of movement. This principle of proportionality requires the collection of information to be adequate, relevant, and for legitimate purposes. The issue has already been raised by the EU Data Protection Working Party, which has questioned the fundamental legitimacy of collecting such information, suggesting that these measures have so far failed to satisfy requirements of security, necessity, and proportionality.

Second, policymakers who believe biometric identity cards prevent illegal migrants from working or claiming benefits need to remember that "clandestine" migrants live and work clandestinely. In the same way, smuggled migrants have little use for identity travel documents, biometric or otherwise. If current methods are failing, it must be questioned whether this is really a result of a lack of technological advancement.

Finally, there is an urgent need to approach immigration reform and anti-terrorism as two separate and distinct issues. The proportionality principle could be invoked by data protection bodies and civil rights advocates with greater authority to gauge the suitability of biometric data collection and usage. In addition, proportionality could make it easier to assess if the measures undertaken are effective enough to justify radical inroads into privacy rights.

## Sources

"BMA calls for safeguards on ID cards" (23 November 2004).

Commission of the European Communities, Extended Impact Assessment (28 December 2004). "Proposal for a Regulation of the European Parliament and of the Council concerning the Visa Information System (VIS) and the exchange of data between member states on short-term visas." COM(2004) 835 final, Brussels: the European Commission.

The Delegation of the European Commission (21 December 2004). "Data protection in the area of Justice, Freedom and Security Meeting with the Joint Supervisory Authorities under the Third Pillar."

EurActive, Justice and Security (10 November 2004). "Hague Programme, JHA programme, 2005 – 10."

European Commission, Information Society website. "Data Protections."

European Union, IDABC (5 April 2004). "U.S. Administration extends US VISIT programme to visa waiver countries."

International Safe Harbor privacy principles.

*Le Monde* (3 December 2004). "Les étrangers sont les premières victimes des violences policières."

Rosenzweig, Paul, Alane Kochems, and Ari Schwartz (21 June 2004). "Biometric Technologies: Security, Legal, and Policy Implications." Legal Memorandum No 12, Heritage Foundation.

*The Somaliland Times* (22 January 2004). "Biometrics to be Used in UK to Tackle Asylum abuse." Issue 105.

Statewatch Bulletin (November-December 2004). "France: Police Brutality escapes punishment." Vol. 14, No. 6.

UK Home Office (8 July 2003). "Visa Fingerprint

## Periodical and Internet Sources Bibliography

*The following articles have been selected to supplement the diverse views presented in this chapter.*

Deborah Amos, "The Hopes (Security) and Fears (Bears) of Syrian Refugees in New Jersey," NPR, September 17, 2016. http://www .npr.org/sections/parallels/2016/09/17/494069828/the-hopes -security-and-fears-bears-of-syrian-refugees-in-new-jersey.

Russell Berman, "Can Terrorists Really Infiltrate the Syrian Refugee Program?, *Atlantic*, November 18, 2015. http://www.theatlantic .com/politics/archive/2015/11/can-terrorists-really-infiltrate-the -syrian-refugee-program/416475.

Alex Bollfrass, Andrew Shaver, and Yang-Yang Zhou, "Don't Fear Refugees: Why They Pose Little Threat to National Security," *Foreign Affairs*, December 9, 2015. https://www.foreignaffairs .com/articles/united-states/2015-12-09/dont-fear-refugees.

Apostolis Fotiadis, "New Security on Greek Islands Reduces Access," *NewsDeeply*, June 15, 2016. https://www.newsdeeply.com /refugees/community/2016/06/15/new-security-on-greek- islands-reduces-access.

Lauren Gambino, "Trump and Syrian Refugees in the US: Separating the Facts from Fiction," *Guardian*, September 2, 2016. https:// www.theguardian.com/us-news/2016/sep/02/donald-trump -syria-refugees-us-immigration-security-terrorism.

Human Rights First, "National Security Voices on Refugee Resettlement: Fact Sheet." http://www.humanrightsfirst.org/sites /default/files/fact-sheet-national-security-validators-refugees.pdf.

Donald Kerwin, "Treating Syrian Refugees as a National Security Threat: Do the Means Fit the End?" Center for Migration Studies, January 18, 2016. http://cmsny.org/publications/kerwin-syrians -national-security.

Karanja Kibicho, "As the Kenyan Minister for National Security, Here's Why I'm Shutting the World's Biggest Refugee Camp," *Independent*, May 9, 2016. http://www.independent.co.uk/voices /as-the-kenyan-minister-for-national-security-heres-why-im -shutting-the-worlds-biggest-refugee-camp-a7020891.html.

Edwin S. Rubenstein, "The Impact of Refugees on the Size and Security of the U.S. Population," Negative Population Growth, Inc., 2016. http://www.npg.org/wp-content/uploads/2016/05 /Impact-of-Refugees2016rev.pdf.

Anne Speckhard, "Taking in Refugees Is Not a Risk to National Security," *Time*, September 9, 2015. http://time.com/4024473 /taking-in-refugees-is-not-a-risk-to-national-security.

OPPOSING
VIEWPOINTS®
SERIES

# CHAPTER 3

# How Much Does the US Economy Rely on Immigrant Labor?

# Chapter Preface

O ne of the most contentious arguments regarding immigration has to do with the economy. Are immigrants, and particularly illegal immigrants, a drain on the US economy, or are they a boon to it? Although one would imagine there would be clear data to easily answer this question, the reality is much more complex. First of all, it is very difficult to compile accurate data on illegal immigrants because they are often too fearful of being turned over to US Immigration and Customs Enforcement to respond to census questions, to file reports with the police, or to use other services.

But an additional problem arises even if accurate data can be amassed. Because immigration has become such a highly politicized—and divisive—topic in the United States, even seemingly "hard" data can be interpreted in different ways. For example, a conservative anti-immigration organization such as the Center for Immigration Studies (CIS) can take the same data set as the progressive pro-immigration organization Center for American Progress (CAP) and yet come up with very different conclusions. Oftentimes, data that falls outside of one research organization's belief system can be ignored and left out of final reports. As Bryan Caplan, echoing Alex Nowrasteh, argues in a viewpoint in this chapter, it can be easy to "cherry-pick" data and provide a one-sided argument of the immigration debate to fit one's ideological biases.

However, nonpartisan studies do exist that can provide a more comprehensive picture of immigration's effect on the economy. In one oft-cited study, the nonpartisan Congressional Budget Office concluded in 2007 that, while undocumented workers do cost local and state governments to an extent, these costs are minor and are largely offset by the taxes that these people pay. This does not include the economic stimulation immigrants might provide through their labor and only focuses on the benefits that are provided to immigrants and the overall costs incurred by local and state governments.

Thus, the answer to this contentious question might be somewhat anti-climactic. While illegal immigrants may cost a modest amount for local and state governments due to the services that they use, this net cost might be completely negated by the labor power they inject into the economy and the taxes they pay. Partisans on both sides, then, might be overstating the facts for explosive rhetoric that is not at all tied to the reality of the situation.

> *"Immigrant advocates say it's hard to make assumptions about how much public services they consume since some undocumented immigrants are afraid to call the police, go to the hospital or use other services because they fear being turned over to immigration officials."*

# Economists Disagree About the Impact of Immigrants on the US Economy

*Becky W. Evans*

*In the following viewpoint, Becky W. Evans describes different studies that examine whether or not illegal immigrants hurt or help America's economy. Unfortunately, as the author states, many of these studies are unreliable due to the political nature of the topic. One researcher profiled, however, states that even if there are costs associated with illegal immigrants, they pay large amounts into the system, both through taxes and labor. Contrary to popular belief, increasing numbers of illegal immigrants are paying taxes despite the fact that they are restricted from many government benefit programs. Evans is a journalist whose writing has appeared in the* Boston Herald, Atlanta Journal-Constitution, *and* Boston Magazine.

As you read, consider the following questions:

1. Why might there be contradicting studies about the economic effect of illegal immigrants?
2. What is an Individual Taxpayer Identification Number?
3. Why might increasing numbers of illegal immigrants be paying taxes?

O ne of the most contentious issues in the immigration debate is whether illegal immigrants create a net loss or a net gain for local, state and federal government coffers.

To answer the question, one needs to know how much illegal immigrants contribute to the government through income, sales, property and other taxes; and how much they cost the government in using public services such as education, health care and law enforcement. Acquiring that information is not easy.

"I think it's very difficult to do that equation, because of all the intangibles that go into someone being in the economy and someone relying on society for different services," said New Bedford Mayor Scott W. Lang.

Numerous academic institutions, government agencies, think tanks and advocacy groups have published reports on the fiscal impact of illegal immigrants on local and state budgets. (None of the studies has focused on New Bedford or Massachusetts.) The studies, which use different methodologies, offer a variety of findings that make it difficult to draw a single conclusion.

For example, a 2006 report by the Texas Office of the Comptroller found that the state's estimated 1.4 million undocumented immigrants contributed more in state revenues than they cost in state services during fiscal year 2005. The net gain for the state was $424.7 million, according to the report. The same study found the opposite trend for local governments and hospitals, which experienced an estimated net loss of $928.9 million in 2005 due to undocumented immigrants.

The findings in the comptroller's study contradict an earlier report published in 2005 by the Federation for American Immigration Reform, a Washington, D.C.-based non-profit groups that aims to stop illegal immigration. That report concluded that illegal immigrants in Texas created an annual fiscal burden of $3.7 billion.

The Congressional Budget Office, which provides Congress with nonpartisan research on budget issues, reviewed 29 such reports published over the past 15 years. It concluded in a 2007 paper that the reports "were not a suitable basis for developing an aggregate national effect across all states," due to a lack of reliable and consistent data and other factors.

The report, entitled "The Impact of Unauthorized Immigrants on the Budgets of State and Local Governments," offered four general conclusions:

- State and local governments incur costs for providing services to unauthorized immigrants and have limited options for avoiding or minimizing those costs.
- The amounts that state and local governments spend on services for unauthorized immigrants represent a small percentage of the total amount spent by those governments to provide such services to residents in their jurisdiction.
- The tax revenues that unauthorized immigrants generate for state and local governments do not offset the total cost of services provided to those immigrants.
- Federal aid programs offer resources to state and local governments that provide services to unauthorized immigrants, but those funds do not fully cover the costs incurred by those governments.

The net fiscal impact of illegal immigrants on a town or state can fluctuate depending on what public services researchers choose to include in the equation, said Steven A. Camarota, director of research at the Center for Immigration Studies in Washington, D.C. The non-profit, non-partisan research

# ILLEGAL IMMIGRANTS ARE AN ASSET TO AMERICA

In response to Walt Back's recent letter ["1965 Immigration Bill Broken," Jan. 6], our immigration system is broken. I definitely agree with him on that point. As an immigration attorney of eight years I have seen the consequences of that broken system firsthand.

But the "enforcement at all costs" and "deport them all" strategies that some advocate would significantly, and possibly devastatingly, affect our economy. Currently there are an estimated 8 million undocumented workers representing more than 5 percent of the U.S. labor force. What would Florida do?

Undocumented workers labor in the citrus groves, strawberry and tomato fields and despite record levels of unemployment, U.S. citizens are not willing to, or capable of, taking on these jobs. According to the nonpartisan Congressional Budget Office, an overhaul of the immigration system that includes legalization would boost the economy with a cumulative $1.5 trillion in added GDP over 10 years.

America has long recognized that strengthening our families is a core national value and interest, and we must continue our historic commitment to bringing families together through our immigration policy. According to a 2012 U.S. Chamber of Commerce report, many small businesses are run by immigrants who came to the United States through the family immigration system, and many of those immigrants become entrepreneurs. These are the businesses that promote the renewal of city neighborhoods and commercial districts, while immigrants and their families strengthen communities and bring diversity to local cultural resources.

The United States was founded by immigrants, and we owe our continued success to their hard work and entrepreneurial spirit. Do we still have room for the next Albert Einstein, Bob Hope or Henry Kissinger?

organization has a "pro-immigrant, low-immigration vision which seeks fewer immigrants but a warmer welcome for those admitted," according to the group's Web site.

If researchers include only direct services such as health care, education and incarceration, the net fiscal impact "tends to come out more positive," Dr. Camarota said. Once you begin to account for the U.S.-citizen children of illegal immigrants and population-based services such as repairs to roads, bridges and other infrastructure, "it turns very negative, very fast," he said.

Randy Capps, a senior researcher at the Washington, D.C.-based Urban Institute, agrees that the net fiscal impact of illegal immigrants varies depending on how you measure taxes and service costs. The Urban Institute is a non-profit, non-partisan policy research and educational organization that aims "to promote sound social policy and public debate on national priorities," according to the group's Web site.

"To me, there is one simple bottom line," Dr. Capps said. "There probably are costs, but they are not that big because undocumented immigrants pay taxes. And the costs are much smaller compared to the economic benefits."

The money that illegal immigrants spend on goods and services in their local communities and around the state "reverberates throughout the whole economy, creates more jobs, more spending and more revenue," he said. "The scale of economic benefit far outweighs any costs on the fiscal side."

Dr. Capps co-authored a 2007 study on immigrants in Arkansas. The study, which was funded by the Winthrop Rockefeller Foundation, found that the total economic impact of Arkansas' 100,000 immigrants (of which 51 percent are undocumented) on the state economy is nearly $3 billion. The Texas Comptroller study found that the 1.4 million undocumented immigrants living in Texas in 2005 contributed $17.7 billion to the state economy.

Dr. Camarota discounts the theory that illegal immigrants have a large economic impact. Because illegal immigrants are generally less-educated than most Americans, and therefore earn lower wages, they don't actually contribute that much to the economy, he said.

"You can't get a big boost to the economy by having a lot of less-educated people coming into the United States, because they don't get paid that much," he said.

When thinking about the fiscal impact of illegal immigrants, it is important to realize that contrary to popular myth, illegal immigrants pay many local, state and federal taxes, said Marcia Hohn, executive director of the Immigrant Learning Center, an advocacy group in Malden that provides free English classes to adult immigrants and refugees.

"There are lots of hidden taxes that immigrants are paying," Ms. Hohn said.

She said it is difficult for illegal immigrants to avoid paying sales and excise taxes for goods and services and property taxes on real estate, whether they rent or own a home. Those who work above the table contribute to the Social Security trust fund by paying payroll taxes.

The Internal Revenue Service and state officials report that an increasing number of undocumented workers are paying federal and state income taxes using an Individual Taxpayer Identification Number, or ITIN, rather than a Social Security Number. An ITIN is a tax processing number issued by the Internal Revenue Service regardless of a person's immigration status.

"ITINs are used for tax purposes only, and are not intended to serve any other purpose," according to the agency. "IRS issues ITINs to help individuals comply with U.S. tax laws, and to provide a means to efficiently process and account for tax returns and payments for those not eligible for Social Security Numbers."

Corinn Williams, executive director of the Community Economic Development Center of Southeastern Massachusetts, said she is amazed at the number of local immigrants who applied for ITINs this year. She said those who are undocumented "want to be up to date and squared away with the IRS" in case immigration policy changes and they are allowed to apply for legal status.

Calculating the costs of illegal immigrants to states and municipalities is as complicated as calculating their fiscal contributions. Many illegal immigrants take advantage of numerous free public services from health care to police and fire protection to schooling for their children. Immigrant advocates say it's hard to make assumptions about how much public services they consume since some undocumented immigrants are afraid to call the police, go to the hospital or use other services because they fear being turned over to immigration officials.

As for federal and state public assistance programs, illegal immigrants qualify for some but not all benefits. For example, undocumented immigrants do not qualify for the same benefits that U.S. citizens get with regards to food stamps, cash assistance and MassHealth, according to the Web-site MassResources.org, a non-government that provides information about federal and state-funded programs.

> *"Apologists for illegal aliens are trying to convince policymakers that it would be better to give those residing here illegally permanent access to U.S. jobs rather than working to remove them from the country and free up those jobs for unemployed U.S. citizens and legal foreign workers."*

# Illegal Immigration Costs US Taxpayers Billions of Dollars Each Year

*Jack Martin and Eric A. Ruark*

*In the following viewpoint, Jack Martin and Eric A. Ruark estimate the costs of illegal immigration to the American government to be approximately $113 billion. However, it is important to note potential conflicts of interest or problems with the collection and interpretation of data used in this study. This report comes from Fair Horizon Press, which is a trademark of the Federation for American Immigration Reform (FAIR), a group that aims to further secure America's border and to stop illegal immigration. As the previous viewpoint made clear, politically motivated reports, such as these, on the subject of immigration are not as reliable (even though they cite many statistics and figures) as non-partisan sources. Martin is director of special projects and Ruark is director of research at the Federation for Immigration Reform.*

"The Fiscal Burden of Illegal Immigration on US Taxpayers (Revised 2013)," by Jack Martin and Eric A. Ruark, Federation for American Immigration Reform. Reprinted by permission.

As you read, consider the following questions:

1. What does the author of this report mean when he uses the term "apologists" for immigration activists?
2. What is the most convincing data provided in this report?
3. What is the least convincing data provided?

## Executive Summary

This report estimates the annual costs of illegal immigration at the federal, state and local level to be about $113 billion; nearly $29 billion at the federal level and $84 billion at the state and local level. The study also estimates tax collections from illegal alien workers, both those in the above-ground economy and those in the underground economy. Those receipts do not come close to the level of expenditures and, in any case, are misleading as an offset because over time unemployed and underemployed U.S. workers would replace illegal alien workers.

## Key Findings

- Illegal immigration costs U.S. taxpayers about $113 billion a year at the federal, state and local level. The bulk of the costs—some $84 billion—are absorbed by state and local governments.
- The annual outlay that illegal aliens cost U.S. taxpayers is an average amount per native-headed household of $1,117. The fiscal impact per household varies considerably because the greatest share of the burden falls on state and local taxpayers whose burden depends on the size of the illegal alien population in that locality
- Education for the children of illegal aliens constitutes the single largest cost to taxpayers, at an annual price tag of nearly $52 billion. Nearly all of those costs are absorbed by state and local governments.

- At the federal level, about one-third of outlays are matched by tax collections from illegal aliens. At the state and local level, an average of less than 5 percent of the public costs associated with illegal immigration is recouped through taxes collected from illegal aliens.
- Most illegal aliens do not pay income taxes. Among those who do, much of the revenues collected are refunded to the illegal aliens when they file tax returns. Many are also claiming tax credits resulting in payments from the U.S. Treasury.

With many state budgets in deficit, policymakers have an obligation to look for ways to reduce the fiscal burden of illegal migration. California, facing a budget deficit of $14.4 billion in 2010-2011, is hit with an estimated $21.8 billion in annual expenditures on illegal aliens. New York's $6.8 billion deficit is smaller than its $9.5 billion in yearly illegal alien costs.

The report examines the likely consequences if an amnesty for the illegal alien population were adopted similar to the one adopted in 1986. The report notes that while tax collections from the illegal alien population would likely increase only marginally, the new legal status would make them eligible for receiving Social Security retirement benefits that would further jeopardize the future of the already shaky system. An amnesty would also result in this large population of illegal aliens becoming eligible for numerous social assistance programs available for low-income populations for which they are not now eligible. The overall result would, therefore, be an accentuation of the already enormous fiscal burden.

# Federal Expenditures on Illegal Aliens

### EDUCATION

| | | |
|---|---|---|
| Title I Program | $1,332,900,000 | |
| Migrant Education Program | $236,900,000 | |
| Title III Program | $538,000,000 | |
| Education Subtotal | | $2,107,800,000 |

### MEDICAL

| | | |
|---|---|---|
| Emergency Medical Care | $250,000,000 | |
| Fraudulent Use of Medicaid | $1,235,000,000 | |
| Medicaid Cost of Childbirth | $1,238,100,000 | |
| Medicaid for Children | $1,626,800,000 | |
| Other Medical Outlays | $1,600,000,000 | |
| Medical Subtotal | | $5,949,900,000 |

### LAW ENFORCEMENT

| | | |
|---|---|---|
| SCAAP Compensation | $330,000,000 | |
| Federal Incarceration | $678,400,000 | |
| Byrne Grants | $24,300,000 | |
| Detention and Removal | $2,545,000,000 | |
| Project Safe Neighborhoods | $39,500,000 | |
| Residual ICE Functions | $2,824,000,000 | |
| Exec. Office of Immigration Review | $222,500,000 | |
| Southwest Border Prosecution | $33,000,000 | |
| National Guard | $642,000,000 | |
| Coast Guard | $500,000,000 | |
| Law Enforcement Subtotal | | $7,838,700,000 |

### PUBLIC ASSISTANCE

| | | |
|---|---|---|
| Free and Reduced Meal Program | $2,264,600,000 | |
| Temporary Asst. Needy Families | $1,030,000,000 | |
| Housing Assistance Programs | $637,000,000 | |
| Child Care & Development Fund | $633,000,000 | |
| Public Assistant Subtotal | | $4,564,600,000 |
| GENERAL EXPENDITURES | | $8,184,400,000 |
| | | |
| TOTAL | $28,645,400,000 | |

# State/Local Expenditures on Illegal Aliens (in millions of dollars)

| STATE | COST | STATE | COST |
|-------|------|-------|------|
| Alabama | $298 | Montana | $32 |
| Alaska | $139 | Nebraska | $262 |
| Arizona | $2,569 | Nevada | $1,191 |
| Arkansas | $244 | New Hampshire | $123 |
| California | $21,756 | New Jersey | $3,478 |
| Colorado | $1,451 | New Mexico | $608 |
| Connecticut | $957 | New York | $9,479 |
| D.C. | $312 | North Carolina | $2,063 |
| Delaware | $305 | North Dakota | $32 |
| Florida | $5,463 | Ohio | $563 |
| Georgia | $2,399 | Oklahoma | $465 |
| Hawaii | $155 | Oregon | $705 |
| Idaho | $188 | Pennsylvania | $1,378 |
| Illinois | $4,592 | Rhode Island | $278 |
| Indiana | $608 | South Carolina | $391 |
| Iowa | $350 | South Dakota | $33 |
| Kansas | $442 | Tennessee | $547 |
| Kentucky | $280 | Texas | $8,878 |
| Louisiana | $224 | Utah | $453 |
| Maine | $41 | Vermont | $38 |
| Maryland | $1,724 | Virginia | $1,905 |
| Massachusetts | $1,862 | Washington | $1,510 |
| Michigan | $929 | West Virginia | $31 |
| Minnesota | $744 | Wisconsin | $883 |
| Mississippi | $106 | Wyoming | $51 |
| Missouri | $338 | TOTAL | $83,851 |

## Receipts from Illegal Aliens

| TAX CATEGORY | FEDERAL | STATE/LOCAL |
|---|---|---|
| Income | -$2,302,800,000 | $244,200,000 |
| Social Security | $7,000,000,000 | |
| Medicare Tax | $1,637,100,000 | |
| Excise and Miscellaneous | $2,489,700,000 | |
| Employer (FUTA & Income) | $632,600,000 | |
| Property Tax | | $1,378,000,000 |
| Sales Tax | | $2,333,000,000 |
| **TOTAL** | **$9,456,600,000** | **$3,955,200,000** |

# Methodology

All studies assessing the impact of illegal aliens begin with estimates of the size of that population. We use a population of 13 million broken down by state.

In our cost estimates we also include the minor children of illegal aliens born in the United States. That adds another 3.4 million children to the 1.3 million children who are illegal aliens themselves. We include these U.S. citizen children of illegal aliens because the fiscal outlays for them are a direct result of the illegal migration that led to their U.S. birth. We do so as well in the assumption that if the parents leave voluntarily or involuntarily they will take these children with them. The birth of these children and their subsequent medical care represent a large share of the estimated Medicaid and Child Health Insurance Program expenditures associated with illegal aliens.

We use data collected by the federal and state governments on school expenses, Limited English Proficiency enrollment, school meal programs, university enrollment, and other public assistance programs administered at the federal and state level. Estimates of incarceration expenses are based on data collected in the State Criminal Alien Assistance Program in which state and local detention facilities seek federal compensation for the cost of detention of criminal and deportable aliens. Estimates for other administration of justice expenditures are based on data collected from the states by the U.S. Department of Justice. General government expenditures are estimated for other non-enumerated functions of government at both the federal and local level. An example would be the cost of fire departments or the cost of the legislature.

Medical costs that amount to 10 percent of overall state and local outlays on illegal aliens derive from our estimate of the childbirths to illegal alien mothers covered by Medicaid, the subsequent medical insurance and treatment of those children and an estimate of uncompensated cost of emergency medical treatment received by illegal aliens. The latter expenditure estimate is based on state and local government studies of uncompensated medical care.

The tax collections from illegal aliens assume eight million illegal alien workers, one-half of whom are in the underground economy. Those in the above-ground economy are assumed to have an average family income of $31,200 (60 hr. workweek @ $10/hr.) with two children.

## Conclusion

The report notes that today's debate over what to do about illegal aliens places the country at a crossroads. One choice is pursuing a strategy that discourages future illegal migration and increasingly diminishes the current illegal alien population through denial of job opportunities and deportations. The other choice would repeat the unfortunate decision made in 1986 to adopt an amnesty that invited continued illegal migration.

[…]

## Introduction

Apologists for illegal aliens are trying to convince policymakers that it would be better to give those residing here illegally permanent access to U.S. jobs rather than working to remove them from the country and free up those jobs for unemployed U.S. citizens and legal foreign workers. They argue that adoption of an amnesty would be a plus for the U.S. economy.[1]

The argument is that an amnesty would help illegal aliens compete for better jobs, thereby raising the income and the taxes they pay. That argument would appear to make sense until it is understood in terms of against whom they would compete for those better jobs, i.e., U.S. citizens and legal residents. While that competition might benefit employers, it would harm job seekers.

The claimed benefits of an amnesty for the illegal alien workers are misleading. Wages for immigrants did rise after the 1986 amnesty. But so did wages in general. It was an inflationary period.[2] According to the Department of Labor's Bureau of Labor Statistics (BLS), beneficiaries of the Immigration Reform and Control Act (IRCA) amnesty saw inflation adjusted wages rise by a meager 15 percent between 1986 and 1991. Relative to the wage gains of other workers, the legalized workers did not make any gains.[3] Most of the workers—more than three-fifths—remained in the same work that they had before the amnesty.[4] Those who illegally entered the country—rather than being visa overstayers—were least likely to show any employment gain from the amnesty.[5] Even if the economy today were not in recession, the deficit in education, skills, and English capability among illegal alien workers dampens the prospect of their upward job mobility regardless of their legal status.

Estimates of the fiscal costs of illegal migration vary. Dr. Donald Huddle, a Rice University economics professor, published a detailed study in 1995.[6] At that time, the illegal alien population was estimated to be about five million persons. His estimate of the annual fiscal cost of those illegal aliens to the federal, state and local governments was about $33 billion. This impact was partially offset by an estimated $12.6 billion in taxes collected from the illegal aliens by the federal, state and local governments, resulting in a net cost to the American taxpayer of about $20 billion every year. This estimate did not include indirect costs that result from unemployment payments to Americans who lost their jobs to illegal aliens willing to work for lower wages. Nor did it include lost tax collections from those American workers who became unemployed. Separately the study estimated those additional indirect costs from illegal migration at $4.3 billion annually. The Huddle study triggered a flurry of responses that in particular challenged the estimated cost of displaced US workers.

In response to this debate, and at the request of the U.S. Commission on Immigration Reform (the Jordan Commission), a panel of economists and demographers was convened by the National Academy of Sciences to provide an estimate of the "Economic, Demographic, and Fiscal Effects of Immigration." The resulting "The New Americans" study, issued in 1997, unfortunately did not distinguish between legal and illegal immigrants. It did find, however, that, "Wages of native-born Americans with less than a high school education who compete with immigrants may have fallen by some 5 percent over the past 15 years because of this competition."[7] The panel found a marginal fiscal advantage to the federal government from immigrant workers and a larger fiscal cost at the state and local level. Implicit in this finding, because of the disparate fiscal effects of high-wage and low-wage workers, was the fact that illegal migration is a net fiscal burden.

A study published by the Center for Immigration Studies (CIS) in 2004 found, "Households headed by illegal aliens imposed more than $26.3 billion in costs on the federal government in 2002 and paid only $16 billion in taxes, creating an annual net fiscal deficit of almost $10.4 billion, or $2,700 per household."[8]

The Heritage Foundation published a fiscal cost study in 2007 that found, "On average, low-skill immigrant households [used as a surrogate for illegal immigrant households] received $30,160 per household in immediate government benefits and services in FY 2004, including direct benefits, means-tested benefits, education, and population-based services. By contrast, low-skill immigrant households paid only $10,573 in taxes. Thus, lowskill immigrant households received nearly three dollars in benefits and services for each dollar in taxes paid."[9]

There were also several state fiscal cost studies that date back to the early 1990s, notably one providing fiscal cost estimates for seven states done by the Urban Institute.[10] The latter study, commissioned by the federal government, was a response to the fact that the illegal immigrant population was by then estimated to have surpassed the size of the population legalized by the 1986 IRCA amnesty, and several of the heavily impacted states had sued the federal government for compensation for the unfair burden they were bearing. All of these studies found a net fiscal burden on the states studied.

FAIR began its own state fiscal cost studies in 2004. To date 17 have been published covering 16 states.[11] They, too, have all documented substantial fiscal burdens in each state based only on the estimated costs of education, medical services, and incarceration after accounting for tax collections from the illegal alien population.

More recently, studies by state authorities and by apologists for the illegal aliens have appeared. Some mix together legal and illegal immigrants, as in the "New Americans" study, thereby obscuring the negative impact of illegal aliens. Others limit the scope of the fiscal costs to only illegal aliens themselves and ignore the government benefits received by illegal aliens on behalf of their U.S.-born children. Some studies assume that illegal aliens are permanent residents, and project future earnings and tax payments on generous assumptions about the aliens' and their offspring's future earnings and tax compliance while ignoring the cost of government services they consume.

The following analysis of the fiscal effects of illegal migration at the national and local level is intended to provide updated estimates and to show that the proposal to adopt an amnesty for the current illegal alien population is not only ill-conceived policy, it is also fiscally irresponsible. A corollary conclusion is that government at all levels—federal, state, and local—should be working cooperatively to benefit the U.S. taxpayer and the U.S. worker by eliminating the jobs magnet that attracts illegal immigrants while also encouraging those already here to return to their homelands.

*"Several national studies have estimated that immigration, given its composition in recent decades, has hurt—albeit to differing degrees—the labor market opportunities of the least skilled and experienced U.S. workers. If a policy goal is to improve the prospects of U.S. workers who have not graduated from high school, this research suggests that changing the skill composition of legal immigrants and reducing the flow of unauthorized aliens might be fruitful courses of action."[12] —Congressional Research Service, January 29, 2009*

First, the fiscal costs of illegal migration at the federal level will be examined. That will be followed by a focus on the fiscal costs at the state and local level. In both analyses, an estimate is provided of taxes collected from the illegal alien population that may be seen as a counterbalance to the fiscal costs. The discussion of tax collections from illegal aliens should be understood, however, as not a true offset to the fiscal cost. The reason it is not a true offset is because the tax collection would still exist, and arguably be even greater, if the jobs occupied by the illegal workers were instead filled by legal workers, and some fiscal outlays would decrease.

We have not tried to estimate the fiscal gain that would accrue if unemployed or underemployed American and legal resident workers were employed in the jobs now occupied by illegal alien workers. Nevertheless, it is clear that there is a negative impact on wages and work opportunities for American workers caused by illegal aliens in the workforce.

Our estimate of about 13 million illegal aliens has not changed since 2007 although there certainly has been some flux since that time both upwards and downwards. In 2007, the Department of Homeland Security (DHS) estimated the illegal alien population at 11.78 million. That estimate did not include some categories of aliens we consider to be part of the illegal alien population such as those in the country for less than one year, aliens illegally in the country when they received Temporary Protected Status, and others paroled into the country or fighting removal.

When considering the fiscal impact of illegal migration it should be kept in mind that, in addition to the estimated current illegal alien population, there are additional millions of residents living in the country who were illegal aliens until they benefited from some legalization provision such as the 1986 IRCA amnesty or smaller amnesties for Central Americans or as a result of the Cuban Adjustment Act, or through adjustment of status or some other defense against deportation. For example, there were about 2.8 million beneficiaries of the IRCA amnesty—nearly nine-tenths of whom were from Mexico or Central America, and nearly 87 percent of whom had at most a high school-level education.[13] To the extent that these earlier illegal alien residents have similar fiscal characteristics to today's illegal aliens, e.g., low-wage earnings because of low-educational achievement, it is also likely that they are a continuing drain on the national and state budgets. However, their presence and their fiscal impact may be considered water over the dam. While policymakers debate what measures to take with regard to the current illegal alien population, they do not have the option of deciding what to do about the earlier amnestied illegal aliens. For that reason, we have not included that population in our assessment of the fiscal costs of illegal migration. However, the ongoing fiscal impact is neither negligible nor a lesson that should ignored as a guide to current immigration policy making.

---

*"Cecilia Conrad, Vice President for Academic Affairs and Dean of the College at Pomona College in Claremont, said there is persuasive evidence that immigrants displace native-born workers in low-skill and entry-level jobs. 'This results from a combination of factors: employer preferences and reliance on informal recruitment networks such as asking current workers to refer friends and family,'*

*Conrad said. In addition, once a workplace is dominated by immigrants, language becomes a barrier for black workers who are not bilingual."* —San Bernardino Sun, April 24, 2010[14]

The size of the illegal alien population we use in estimating the fiscal impact includes 3.9 million U.S.-born children of illegal aliens. We recognize that these U.S.-citizen children qualify for a broad range of social assistance programs. But we also judge that responsible parents would take these dual-nationality children with them when they return voluntarily or involuntarily to their homeland. Based on research of the Urban Institute, we use an assumption of about 8.4 million workers in the workforce, of whom about half are in the underground economy, i.e. day laborers, independent contractors, domestics, pieceworkers, etc., and the other half are in the formal economy using fake or stolen identities.[15]

## Endnotes

[1] See for example "report: immigration legalization could boost U.S. economy" Latina media website (http://www.latina.com/lifestyle/news-politics/report-immigration -legalization-could-boost-us-economy, consulted March 16, 2010 )

[2] Inflation during the 5-year period (1986-91) amounted to 24.1 percent—nearly 5 percent per year.

[3] "Effects of the Immigration Reform Control Act: Characteristics and Labor Market Behavior of the Legalized Population Five Years Following Legalization," U.S. Department of Labor, Bureau of International Labor Affairs, May 1996.

[4] "Economic Progress via Legalization: Lessons from the Last Legalization Program," Immigration Policy Center, November 2009.

[5] Rytina, Nancy, "Irca Legalization Effects: Lawful Permanent Residence and Naturalization Through 2001," U.S. Immigration and Naturalization Service, Office of Policy and Planning, October 25, 2002.

[6] Huddle, Donald, "The Net National Costs of Immigration: Fiscal Effects of Welfare Restorations to Legal Immigrants," Carrying Capacity Network, Washington, DC, 1995.

[7] "Report in Brief—The New Americans: Economic, Demographic, and Fiscal Effects of Immigration," National Academy of Sciences, May 1997, Washington, DC.

[8] Camarota, Steven A., "The High Cost of Cheap Labor: Illegal Immigration and the Federal Budget," Center for Immigration Studies, August 2004, Washington DC.

[9] Rector, Robert and Christine Kim, "The Fiscal Cost of Low-Skill Immigrants to the U.S. Taxpayer," May 22, 2007, The Heritage Foundation, Washington DC.

[10] "Fiscal Impacts of Undocumented Aliens: Selected Estimates for Seven States," The Urban Institute, Washington, DC, September 1994.

[11] All of FAIR's state fiscal cost studies are available on FAIR's website at http://www.fairus.org/site/pagenavigator/issues/publications/.

[12] "Immigration: The Effects on Low-Skilled and High-Skilled Native-Born Workers," Congressional Research Service, January 29, 2009.

[13] "Report on the Legalized Alien Population," U.S. Department of Justice, (pub. m-375), March 1992, Washington, DC. This report provided data on nationality and educational level of the amnesty population who claimed residence in the United States since 1992. For the portion of the amnestied population simultaneously benefiting from the separate agricultural worker amnesty provision, our assumption is that all of those beneficiaries had no higher than a high school education.

[14] Job Study: Latinos beating out blacks," *San Bernardino Sun*, April 24, 2010.

[15] Capps, Randolph, et al., "A Profile of the Low-Wage Immigrant Workforce," October 27, 2003, The Urban Institute, Washington, DC. Their estimate of 5.2 million illegal immigrants in the workforce was adjusted upward by the change in size of the illegal alien population.

> *"It is helpful to take a moment to reflect on the important contributions by the generations of immigrants who have helped us build our economy, and made America the economic engine of the world."*

# Ten Ways Immigrants Help Build and Strengthen Our Economy

### Jason Furman and Danielle Gray

*In this viewpoint, the authors argue that immigrants play an important role in positioning America as "the economic engine of the world." According to them, immigration is not a drain on the economy but rather propels our economy forward. They use the following ten reasons to back up why they believe immigrants play such an essential role. Gray was assistant to the president and cabinet secretary during the Obama administration. Furman was the administration's chairman of the Council of Economic Advisers.*

As you read, consider the following questions:

1.  How much do immigrant-owned businesses generate annually?
2.  In which important discipline are immigrants making notable contributions?
3.  Which immigration reform legislation is cited as helping the economy?

America is a nation of immigrants. Our American journey and our success would simply not be possible without the generations of immigrants who have come to our shores from every corner of the globe. It is helpful to take a moment to reflect on the important contributions by the generations of immigrants who have helped us build our economy, and made America the economic engine of the world.

How do immigrants strengthen the U.S. economy? Below is our top 10 list for ways immigrants help to grow the American economy.

1.  **Immigrants start businesses.** According to the Small Business Administration, immigrants are 30 percent more likely to start a business in the United States than non-immigrants, and 18 percent of all small business owners in the United States are immigrants.
2.  **Immigrant-owned businesses create jobs for American workers.** According to the Fiscal Policy Institute, small businesses owned by immigrants employed an estimated 4.7 million people in 2007, and according to the latest estimates, these small businesses generated more than $776 billion annually.
3.  **Immigrants are also more likely to create their own jobs.** According the U.S. Department of Labor, 7.5 percent of the foreign born are self-employed compared to 6.6 percent among the native-born.

4. **Immigrants develop cutting-edge technologies and companies.** According to the National Venture Capital Association, immigrants have started 25 percent of public U.S. companies that were backed by venture capital investors. This list includes Google, eBay, Yahoo!, Sun Microsystems, and Intel.

5. **Immigrants are our engineers, scientists, and innovators.** According to the Census Bureau, despite making up only 16 percent of the resident population holding a bachelor's degree or higher, immigrants represent 33 percent of engineers, 27 percent of mathematicians, statisticians, and computer scientist, and 24 percent of physical scientists. Additionally, according to the Partnership for a New American Economy, in 2011, foreign-born inventors were credited with contributing to more than 75 percent of patents issued to the top 10 patent-producing universities.

6. **Immigration boosts earnings for American workers.** Increased immigration to the United States has increased the earnings of Americans with more than a high school degree. Between 1990 and 2004, increased immigration was correlated with increasing earnings of Americans by 0.7 percent and is expected to contribute to an increase of 1.8 percent over the long-term, according to a study by the University of California at Davis.

7. **Immigrants boost demand for local consumer goods.** The Immigration Policy Center estimates that the purchasing power of Latinos and Asians, many of whom are immigrants, alone will reach $1.5 trillion and $775 billion, respectively, by 2015.

8. **Immigration reform legislation like the DREAM Act reduces the deficit.** According to the nonpartisan Congressional Budget Office, under the 2010 House-passed version of the DREAM Act, the federal deficit would be reduced by $2.2 billion over ten years because of increased tax revenues.

9. **Comprehensive immigration reform would create jobs.**
   Comprehensive immigration reform could support and
   create up to 900,000 new jobs within three years of reform
   from the increase in consumer spending, according to the
   Center for American Progress.

10. **Comprehensive immigration reform would increase
    America's GDP.** The nonpartisan Congressional Budget
    Office found that even under low investment assumptions,
    comprehensive immigration reform would increase GDP by
    between 0.8 percent and 1.3 percent from 2012 to 2016.

As a nation of immigrants, we must remember that generations
of immigrants have helped lay the railroads and build our cities,
pioneer new industries and fuel our Information Age, from
Google to the iPhone. As President Obama said at a naturalization
ceremony held at the White House last week:

> The lesson of these 236 years is clear—immigration makes
> America stronger. Immigration makes us more prosperous. And
> immigration positions America to lead in the 21st century. And
> these young men and women are testaments to that. No other
> nation in the world welcomes so many new arrivals. No other
> nation constantly renews itself, refreshes itself with the hopes,
> and the drive, and the optimism, and the dynamism of each new
> generation of immigrants. You are all one of the reasons that
> America is exceptional. You're one of the reasons why, even after
> two centuries, America is always young, always looking to the
> future, always confident that our greatest days are still to come.

We celebrate the contributions of all Americans to building our
nation and its economy, including the generations of immigrants.

> "*The data presented here make clear that the often-made argument that immigrants only take jobs Americans don't want is simply wrong.*"

# There Are No Jobs Specifically for Immigrants that Natives Do Not Risk Losing

## Steven A. Camarota and Karen Zeigler

*In the following viewpoint, Steven A. Camarota and Karen Zeigler confront the commonly held belief that immigrants typically only do less skilled jobs that Americans don't want. Through examination of data, they find that there are not many majority-immigrant occupations, thus refuting this belief. It is important to know, however, that the organization behind the study, the Center for Immigration Studies (CIS), has previously been cited by non-partisan immigrant-research organizations for "misleading" reports due to the politicization of the data they use. Therefore, it is important to understand possible motives behind supposedly data-driven viewpoints. Camarota is the director of research and Zeigler is a demographer at the Center for Immigration Studies (CIS), a self-stated pro–low immigration research organization.*

"Jobs Americans Won't Do? A Detailed Look at Immigrant Employment by Occupation," by Steven A. Camarota and Karen Zeigler, Center for Immigration Studies, August, 2009. Reprinted by permission.

As you read, consider the following questions:

1. Might there be difficulty using Census Bureau data in such a study if illegal immigrants are often not counted (or do not want to be counted) in the census?
2. What, in your opinion, is the strongest data used here for the purpose of the authors' argument?
3. What is the weakest data used? Why?


This analysis tests the often-made argument that immigrants only do jobs Americans don't want. If the argument is correct, there should be occupations comprised entirely or almost entirely of immigrants. But Census Bureau data collected from 2005 to 2007, which allow for very detailed analysis, show that even before the recession there were only a tiny number of majority-immigrant occupations. (Click here to see detailed table.)

Among the findings:

- Of the 465 civilian occupations, only four are majority immigrant. These four occupations account for less than 1 percent of the total U.S. workforce. Moreover, native-born Americans comprise 47 percent of workers in these occupations.
- Many jobs often thought to be overwhelmingly immigrant are in fact majority native-born:
  - Maids and housekeepers: 55 percent native-born
  - Taxi drivers and chauffeurs: 58 percent native-born
  - Butchers and meat processors: 63 percent native-born
  - Grounds maintenance workers: 65 percent native-born
  - Construction laborers: 65 percent native-born
  - Porters, bellhops, and concierges: 71 percent native-born
  - Janitors: 75 percent native-born
- There are 93 occupations in which 20 percent or more of workers are immigrants. These high-immigrant occupations are primarily, but not exclusively, lower-wage jobs that require relatively little formal education.

- There are 23.6 million natives in these high-immigrant occupations (20 percent or more immigrant). These occupations include 19 percent of all native workers.
- Most natives do not face significant job competition from immigrants; however, those who do tend to be less-educated and poorer than those who face relatively little competition from immigrants.
- In high-immigrant occupations, 57 percent of natives have no more than a high school education. In occupations that are less than 20 percent immigrant, 35 percent of natives have no more than a high school education. And in occupations that are less than 10 percent immigrant, only 26 percent of natives have no more than a high school education.
- In high-immigrant occupations the average wages and salary for natives is one-fourth lower than in occupations that are less than 20 percent immigrant.
- Some may believe that natives in high-immigrant occupations are older and that few young natives are willing to do that kind of work. But 33 percent of natives in these occupations are age 30 or younger. In occupations that are less than 20 percent immigrant, 28 percent of natives are 30 or younger.
- It is worth remembering that not all high-immigrant occupations are lower-skilled and lower-wage. For example, 44 percent of medical scientists are immigrants, as are 34 percent of software engineers, 27 percent of physicians, and 25 percent of chemists.
- It is also worth noting that a number of politically important groups tend to face very little job competition from immigrants. For example, just 10 percent of reporters are immigrants, as are only 6 percent of lawyers and judges and 3 percent of farmers and ranchers.

## Methodology

The data for this analysis are from the public-use file of the combined three-year sample of the American Community Survey (ACS) for 2005 through 2007. This is the first public-use three-year file to be released by the Census Bureau. The public-use file of the ACS is enormous, allowing for detailed analysis by occupation. The sample includes 4.4 million individuals in the civilian non-institutionalized labor force, about 560,000 of whom are immigrants. Persons in the labor force are either working or looking for work. Like almost all the labor force statistics reported by the government, we confine our analysis to civilians 16 years of age and older not in institutions.[1] The immigrant population, which can also be referred to as the foreign-born, is defined as persons living in the United States who were not U.S. citizens at birth. In the ACS this includes people who responded to the survey who are naturalized American citizens, legal permanent residents (green card holders), illegal aliens, and people on long-term temporary visas such as students or guest workers. It does not include those born abroad of American parents or those born in outlying territories of the United States, such as Puerto Rico. Prior research indicates that some 90 percent of illegal immigrants respond to the ACS.[2]

## Discussion

The American economy is dynamic, and it would be a mistake to think that every job taken by an immigrant is a job lost by a native. Many factors impact employment and wages. But it would also be a mistake to assume that dramatically increasing the number of workers in these occupations as a result of immigration policy has no impact on the employment prospects or wages of natives. The data presented here make clear that the often-made argument that immigrants only take jobs Americans don't want is simply wrong. To talk about the labor market as if there were jobs done entirely or almost entirely by immigrants is not helpful to understanding the potential impact of immigration on American workers. It gives

# Exactly Who Feels Threatened by Undocumented Immigrant Laborers?

Economists generally argue that immigration helps the U.S. economy by adding young workers to the workforce. The Brookings Institution's Michael Greenstone and Adam Looney wrote last year that "on average, immigrant workers increase the opportunities and incomes of Americans" while a study released in January by the liberal Center for American Progress concluded that granting legal status to undocumented workers could create jobs.

But such studies have done little to quell fears about whether undocumented immigrants are taking jobs from U.S. citizens. Republicans were more likely to be worried about undocumented workers than Democrats, the Ramussen survey found. Roughly 71 percent of GOP voters and 51 percent of unaffiliated voters said workers without work permits were taking jobs from American citizens, while 31 percent of Democrats said the same.

Men were more likely to fear undocumented workers than women. People over the age of 40 also were more worried about competing for jobs against immigrants without work visas compared with younger respondents. Blacks were less afraid of undocumented workers compared with white voters.

Low-income respondents especially felt threatened by undocumented workers, as did Americans without college degrees, the poll found. The poll of 1,000 likely voters was conducted from Aug. 9-10. The poll explained to respondents that the majority of undocumented workers were low-skilled.

**"Undocumented Immigrants Taking Jobs From US Citizens? Most Americans Believe Immigration Is Bad For Economy," by Cristina Silva, IBT Media Inc., August 14, 2015.**

the false impression that the job market is segmented between jobs that are done almost exclusively by immigrants and jobs that are exclusively native. This is clearly not the case.

This analysis focuses on the nation as a whole; the immigrant shares of occupations will vary significantly at the state and local level. But Americans move around the country a great deal. The 2007 ACS showed that about 38 percent of adult natives live outside the state in which they were born. We live in a national economy in which workers can and do move to higher-wage (relative to cost of living) and lower-unemployment areas over time. If immigration levels were lower and a shortage of workers did develop in one part of the country, higher wages and lower unemployment would, over time, tend to induce Americans to move to these areas. Thus in the long term it makes sense to think of the economy as national in scope.[3]

## End Notes

1 Those who are institutionalized live under formally authorized supervision or care such as those in correctional institutions and nursing homes. Since our focus is occupations we also exclude from our analysis the relatively small number of people who did not provide an occupation.

2 The Department of Homeland Security estimates a 10 percent undercount of illegal aliens in Census Bureau data. See Table 2 in *Estimates of the Unauthorized Immigrant Population Residing in the United States: January 2007* at http://www.dhs.gov/xlibrary/ assets/statistics/publications/ois_ill_pe_20.... DHS estimates of the illegal population are based on the ACS with the assumption that 10 percent of illegal immigrants are missed by the survey.

3 In its 1997 study of immigration's impact on the labor market, the National Research Council concluded that the effects of immigration are likely to be national in scope and not simply confined to high-immigrant areas of the country. See James P. Smith and Barry Edmonston, eds., *The New Americans: Economic, Demographic, and Fiscal Effects of Immigration*

> *"As a number of economists have pointed out, immigrants don't 'do jobs Americans won't do.' They do jobs that wouldn't exist if the immigrants weren't there to do them."*

# Immigrants Do Jobs Natives Won't Do

### Bryan Caplan

*In the following viewpoint, Bryan Caplan argues against the previous viewpoint that immigrants do in fact take on jobs that most native Americans refuse to do. It is important to keep in mind the motives behind each viewpoint based on their affiliation with partisan organizations before reaching your own conclusions about the information presented. This viewpoint uses ample quotations from other sources in order to back up its essential argument. Caplan is a libertarian economics professor at George Mason University and a passionate advocate of open borders.*

As you read, consider the following questions:

1. Do you agree that immigration is "taboo" to talk about? Why or why not?
2. Why would certain jobs not exist if immigrants were not there to do them?
3. Do you find the long quote from Alex Nowrasteh effective in presenting how certain data can be presented in misleading ways in terms of the immigration debate?

One of the arguments offered by supporters of expanded immigration, particularly in the context of low-skilled immigration to the United States, is that "immigrants do jobs that natives won't do." This argument, in the form stated, is incorrect, or at any rate, misleading. However, it does capture a conclusion many economists reach, which some have summarized as: "immigrants do jobs that wouldn't exist if the immigrants weren't there to do them."

This position has been critiqued by many who are critical of immigration. For instance, in a syndicated column titled Immigration Taboos, Thomas Sowell writes:

> Immigration has joined the long list of subjects on which it is taboo to talk sense in plain English. At the heart of much confusion about immigration is the notion that we "need" immigrants—legal or illegal—to do work that Americans won't do.
>
> What we "need" depends on what it costs and what we are willing to pay. If I were a billionaire, I might "need" my own private jet. But I can remember a time when my family didn't even "need" electricity.
>
> Leaving prices out of the picture is probably the source of more fallacies in economics than any other single misconception. At current wages for low-level jobs and current levels of welfare, there are indeed many jobs that Americans will not take.
>
> The fact that immigrants—and especially illegal immigrants—will take those jobs is the very reason the wage levels will not rise enough to attract Americans.
>
> This is not rocket science. It is elementary supply and demand. Yet we continue to hear about the "need" for immigrants to do jobs that Americans will not do—even though these are all jobs that Americans have done for generations before mass illegal immigration became a way of life.

However, the actual economic argument is more subtle, and not so easy to ridicule. The key is to remember that prices not only affect the quantity of labor supply, but also the quantity of labor demand. If the supply curve shrinks inward because immigrants are not allowed in the labor market, then the price of labor increases, but the quantity supplied decreases, so overall, there are fewer jobs and less production. In the article Why Is Immigration Illegal Anyway?, Benjamin Powell and Art Carden say:

> Immigrants tend to be either high-skilled or low-skilled; Americans tend to be more toward the middle of the skill distribution. This means that immigrants aren't substitutes for American labor but, instead, free up American labor to do jobs where it is more productive. That's one reason economists don't find that immigration depresses the wages of the native-born.
>
> As a number of economists have pointed out, immigrants don't "do jobs Americans won't do." They do jobs that wouldn't exist if the immigrants weren't there to do them. By making life harder for a population of undocumented immigrants, the state government has ensured that future generations of Alabamians will be poorer than they would otherwise be.

A blog post by Alex Nowrasteh titled Thomas Sowell on the Economics of Immigration critiqued Sowell for one-sided presentation of the economics of immigration. Here is the relevant quote from Nowrasteh's piece:

> Issues of economic vocabulary aside, Sowell only described one possible outcome from a reduction in the supply of low-skilled immigrant farm workers: an increase in wages. The far more likely reaction is that American farmers will stop growing crops that require many workers. Without a large supply of low-skilled immigrant farm workers, labor-intensive farming would either shrink dramatically or disappear entirely. American farmers would either grow different crops that could be profitably harvested mechanically or stop farming. American consumers would either import fruits and vegetables that require large numbers of workers from countries where those workers are abundant, or scale back their consumption of those food stuffs. Fewer workers also means fewer consumers of these agricultural goods, decreasing demand and partly offsetting some of the increase in price that would occur from a decrease in supply. Those effects would be the economically efficient outcome if

increased labor scarcity was driven by changes in the free market. In this case, however, the increase in labor scarcity would come from legislation mandating such scarcity.

Insights from labor economics help explain why the American growing of fruits and vegetables would diminish if low-skilled immigration was ended. If the marginal value of the worker's production is greater than the wage, it is profitable for a firm to hire that employee. For example, if a worker's marginal value product (MVP) is $10 per hour, it is profitable to employ that worker at a wage of less than $10. (If MVP = wage, the employer is indifferent assuming no transaction costs). Based on the enormous range of work and welfare options open to Americans, farmers would likely have to pay wages so high to attract enough American workers that most labor-intensive agriculture would be unprofitable. Alabama provides an example.

Furthermore, it's hard to see why it's desirable to increase the wages of low-productivity farm workers by increasing their scarcity. Raising the wages in occupations that don't require a high school degree is antithetical to other aspects of public policy that seek to increase the rate of high school graduation (whether or not that is a valid concern for government). There is evidence that more immigration further incentivizes Americans to actually finish high school. The government should not create a policy designed to increase wages for low-skilled farm workers that could drive relatively higher-skilled Americans into those occupations. Since educated workers have more choices in the labor market, the effect of attracting them into lower-productivity professions through changes in policy will likely diminish economic and productivity growth.

Speaking of immigration reform proponents, Sowell states, "They say Americans won't do these jobs. These are jobs Americans have done for generations, if not centuries." In this instance, Sowell cherry-picks his opponent's arguments and chooses to address the ludicrous ones while ignoring those with substance. Americans sailed wind-powered ships around the world and used horses instead of cars for centuries. That, however, is not an argument that a government law should increase the scarcity of modern ships and cars. Sowell is right that

Americans could do these low-skilled agriculture jobs. We could also become hunter-gatherers again. But that does not mean that we should, if cheaper and better options are available. Sowell does not say that we should exclude low-skilled immigrants but his tone and the conspicuous absence of him criticizing economically ignorant arguments from the anti-immigration-reform side are serious indications of his opinions on the issue.

Furthermore, Sowell is right that the economy would adjust to a decrease in the supply of low-skilled labor, but he fails to mention that it would do so by shrinking. The economy would likewise adjust if the American government declared that electricity was illegal or all imports were banned. Arguing that the economy would adjust to artificially created scarcity does not justify creating such scarcity through government fiat.

Immigration restrictions increase labor scarcity, especially in niches of the labor market where relatively few Americans work. The main effect of increasing labor scarcity by further restricting the supply of low-skilled immigrant workers will not be to raise the wages of Americans, thereby drawing them to pick crops; it would be to kill large portions of the agricultural sector and other portions of the economy that demand large numbers of relatively low-skilled workers to operate most efficiently and profitably.

> *"Common-sense reform would restore public faith in the system and level the playing field for all Americans, while supercharging the economic benefits from our immigrant population."*

# The Facts Show Immigrants Benefit Our Economy

## The Center for American Progress (CAP) Immigration Team

*In the following viewpoint, the CAP Immigration Team presents data to show that immigration has been a "constant source of economic vitality and demographic dynamism throughout our nation's history." Yet, as the CAP team argues, the immigration system is broken and needs to be fixed. This is because there are few paths to citizenship for undocumented workers in the United States. Thus, a legal path to immigration would be "common sense" and would only help further strengthen the American economy, according to this viewpoint. The Center for American Progress is a progressive research institution that aims for "common-sense" immigration reform.*

"The Facts on Immigration Today," by The CAP Immigration Team, Center for American Progress, October 23, 2014. Reprinted by permission.

As you read, consider the following questions:

1. What is the difference regarding gender, compared to immigration statistics of the past?
2. How do the costs of inaction and strict border enforcement measure up?
3. How much does deporting one individual cost taxpayers?

Immigration has been a constant source of economic vitality and demographic dynamism throughout our nation's history. Immigrants are taxpayers, entrepreneurs, job creators, and consumers. But the immigration system is broken and in need of an overhaul.

Although the U.S. border is now more secure than ever, decades of ever-increasing border and interior enforcement have exacerbated the dysfunction caused by rigid, out-of-date laws. Immigration reform that comprehensively addresses these systemic problems—including providing a pathway to citizenship for undocumented immigrants living and working in the United States—is supported by large swaths of Americans. Common-sense reform would restore public faith in the system and level the playing field for all Americans, while supercharging the economic benefits from our immigrant population.

Below are the latest and most essential facts about immigrants and immigration reform in our nation today.

[…]

## Today's immigrant population

### Foreign-born population

- **The foreign-born population consisted of 40.7 million people in 2012.** Broken down by immigration status, the foreign-born population was composed of 18.6 million naturalized U.S. citizens and 22.1 million noncitizens in 2012. Of the noncitizens, approximately 13.3 million were legal permanent residents, 11.3 million were unauthorized migrants, and 1.9 million were on temporary visas.

- **The past decade saw a significant increase in the foreign-born population.** Between 2000 and 2012, there was a 31.2 percent increase in the foreign-born population. During this period, the immigrant population grew from 31.1 million to 40.8 million people.
- **The foreign-born share of the U.S. population has more than doubled since the 1960s, but it is still below its all-time high.** The immigrant population was 5.4 percent of the total U.S. population in 1960. By 2012, immigrants made up 13 percent of the total U.S. population. Still, today's share of the immigrant population as a percentage of the total U.S. population remains below its peak in 1890, when 14.8 percent of the U.S. population had immigrated to the country.
- **The countries of origin of today's immigrants are more diverse than they were 50 years ago.** In 1960, a full 75 percent of the foreign-born population that resided in the United States came from Europe, while in 2012, only 11.8 percent of the immigrant population emigrated from Europe. In 2012, 11.6 million foreign-born residents—28 percent of the foreign-born population—came from Mexico; 2.3 million immigrants came from China; 2 million came from India; 1.9 million came from the Philippines; 1.3 million came from both Vietnam and El Salvador; and 1.1 million came from both Cuba and Korea.
- **Immigrants today are putting down roots across the United States, in contrast to trends seen 50 years ago.** In the 1960s, two-thirds of U.S. states had populations in which less than 5 percent of individuals were foreign born. The opposite is true today: In 2012, 61 percent of the foreign-born population lived in the West and the South—a dramatic departure from trends 50 years ago, when 70 percent of the immigrant population lived in the Northeast and Midwest.

- **Today, women outnumber men in the foreign-born population.** In 2012, 51.4 percent of the U.S. immigrant population was female. Until the 1960s, immigrant men outnumbered immigrant women. However, by the 1970s, the number of female immigrants had surpassed the number of male immigrants.

- **The foreign-born population is, on average, slightly older than the native-born population.** In 2012, the median age for all foreign-born people was 42, while the median age for all native-born people was 35.

- **There are almost 1 million lesbian, gay, bisexual, and transgender, or LGBT, adult immigrants in the United States today.** The estimated 904,000 LGBT adult immigrants are more likely to be young and male compared with the overall immigrant population.

- **Immigrants have diverse educational backgrounds.** In 2012, 11.6 percent of immigrants had a master's degree, professional degree, or doctorate degree, compared with 10.8 percent of the native-born population. That same year, 69.4 percent of the foreign-born population had attained a high school diploma, GED, or higher, compared with 89.9 percent of the native-born population.

- **More than half of the foreign-born population are homeowners.** In 2012, 51 percent of immigrant heads of household owned their own homes, compared with 66 percent of native-born heads of household. Among immigrants, 65 percent of naturalized citizens owned their own homes in 2012.

- **Less than one in five immigrants live in poverty, and they are no more likely to use social services than the native-born Americans.** In 2012, 19.1 percent of immigrants lived in poverty, while 15.4 percent of the native-born population lived in poverty. Of the foreign born, the two largest groups living in poverty were the 3.2 million people who emigrated from Mexico and the 1.4 million people who emigrated from either South or East Asia. Despite of this, studies have consistently shown that immigrants use social programs such as Medicaid and Supplemental Security Income at similar rates to native households.

- **The 20 million U.S.-born children of immigrants are significantly better off financially than their immigrant parents.** The median annual household income of second-generation Americans in 2012 was $58,100, just $100 below the national average. This was significantly higher than the median annual household income of their parents at $45,800.

- **U.S.-born children of immigrants are more likely to go to college, less likely to live in poverty, and equally likely to be homeowners as the average American.** About 36 percent of U.S.-born children of immigrants are college graduates—5 percent above the national average. Eleven percent of U.S.-born children of immigrants live in poverty— well below the national average of 13 percent. And around 64 percent of them are homeowners, just 1 percent below the national average.

- **Immigrants are less likely to commit crimes or to be incarcerated than native-born Americans.** A 2007 study by the Immigration Policy Center found that the incarceration rate for immigrant men ages 18 to 39 in 2000 was 0.7 percent, while the incarceration rate for native-born men of the same age group was 3.5 percent. While the foreign-born share of the U.S. population grew from 8 percent to 13 percent between 1990 and 2010, FBI data indicate that violent crime rates across the country fell by about 45 percent, while property crime rates fell by 42 percent.

## Undocumented immigrant population

- **The undocumented population has stayed relatively stable, after declining slightly during the Great Recession.** In 2000, there were an estimated 8.4 million undocumented people residing in the United States. This population peaked in

2007 at 12 million but saw a gradual decline during the Great Recession. In 2012, an estimated 11.7 million undocumented immigrants resided in the United States. Since then, the numbers have stabilized. By the end of 2012, there were approximately 11.2 million undocumented immigrants in the United States, and that number remained constant into 2013 with 11.3 million undocumented immigrants.

- **People from Mexico account for a large part of the undocumented population living in the United States, but their share has diminished in recent years.** In 2012, 6 million people—or 52 percent of the undocumented population—were from Mexico, down from the peak of 6.9 million—or 57 percent—in 2007.

- **Six states are home to the majority of the undocumented population.** As of 2012, 22 percent of the nation's undocumented population lives in California. Fifteen percent lives in Texas, 8 percent lives in Florida, 7 percent lives in New York, 4 percent lives in Illinois, and 4 percent lives in New Jersey.

- **The majority of undocumented immigrants are long-term residents, committed to living in the United States.** In 2013, the median length of residence for unauthorized immigrants in the United States was 13 years, at least 5 years longer than it had been in 2003. Currently, 62 percent of undocumented immigrants have been living in the United States for 10 years or longer, and a full 88 percent have been living in the United States for five years or longer.

- **Many undocumented immigrants could be sponsored for a green card but cannot adjust their status because they are presently undocumented.** Hundreds of thousands of undocumented immigrants could qualify for a green card by virtue of having a relative who is a U.S. citizen, but—because of bars to re-entering the United States that were put in place in 1996—most would have to leave the United States for a period of at least 10 years before becoming eligible to reunite with their families.

- **Undocumented immigrants are often part of the same family as documented immigrants.** 16.6 million people were in "mixed-status" families—those with at least one undocumented immigrant—in 2011. Nine million of these families had at least one U.S.-born child.

- **Nearly half of the undocumented population has minor children, many of them born in the United States.** In 2012, 4.7 million undocumented adults were parents of minor children, including 3.8 million whose children were U.S. citizens.

- **One in five undocumented immigrant adults has a U.S. citizen or lawful permanent resident spouse.** Of the 10 million adult undocumented immigrants living in the United States in 2012, approximately 767,000 were married to a U.S. citizen and 944,000 were married to a lawful permanent resident.

- **Undocumented immigrants comprise a disproportionately large percentage of the labor force relative to the size of the overall population.** In 2010, 8.4 million undocumented immigrants were employed in the United States. They represented 5.2 percent of the U.S. labor force, although they comprised only 3.7 percent of the U.S. population.

- **There are more than a quarter of a million LGBT undocumented adult immigrants in the United States today.** The estimated 267,000 LGBT undocumented adult immigrants as of 2013 are more likely to be male and younger relative to all undocumented immigrants. Around 71 percent of LGBT undocumented adults are Hispanic, and 15 percent are Asian American or Pacific Islander.

- **Nearly half of settled undocumented immigrants are homeowners.** Among undocumented immigrants who had lived in the United States for 10 years or longer, 45 percent were homeowners in 2008. Among undocumented immigrants who had lived in the United States for less than 10 years, 27 percent were homeowners in 2008.

- **More than half of the undocumented immigrant population has a high school degree or higher.** According to a 2009 Pew Research Center's Hispanic Trends Project study, 52 percent of undocumented immigrants have a high school diploma or higher and 15 percent have a bachelor's degree or higher.

[...]

## Immigrants and the economy

### The economic imperative for immigration reform

- **Legalization and naturalization of undocumented immigrants would bolster their wages.** The annual income of unauthorized immigrants would be 15.1 percent higher within five years if they were granted legal status. In addition, if undocumented immigrants earned their citizenship, their wages would rise by an additional 10 percent. This wage increase would occur because legal status provides the undocumented legal protections, grants access to better jobs, promotes investments in education and training, and fosters small-business creation.
- **Immigration reform would increase the earnings of all Americans.** Immigration reform that includes a pathway to citizenship for undocumented immigrants in five years would increase the earnings of all American workers by $618 billion over the next decade.
- **Permitting undocumented immigrants to gain legal status and citizenship would expand economic growth.** Naturalized workers earn higher wages, consume more goods and services, and pay more in taxes, which in turn creates economic growth. If the undocumented immigrants in our nation were granted legal status today and citizenship in five

years, the 10-year cumulative increase in U.S. gross domestic product, or GDP, would be $1.1 trillion.

- **Granting citizenship to undocumented immigrants would create jobs and increase tax revenues.** If undocumented immigrants acquired legal status today and citizenship in five years, the economy would add an average of 159,000 new jobs per year, and formerly unauthorized workers would pay an additional $144 billion in federal, state, and local taxes over a 10-year period.

- **Immigration reform would translate into a significant decrease in the federal budget deficit.** The nonpartisan Congressional Budget Office, or CBO, found that S. 744—the Border Security, Economic Opportunity, and Immigration Modernization Act, as passed by the Senate—would reduce the budget deficit by $135 billion in the first decade after the bill's passage and by an additional $685 billion in the second decade, when most undocumented immigrants would become eligible for citizenship.

- **Citizenship would allow millions of undocumented immigrants to work on the books and contribute to Social Security.** If undocumented immigrants gained legal status and citizenship, they would provide a net $606.4 billion contribution to Social Security over the next 36 years—the same time period when retiring Baby Boomers will place the greatest strain on the system. These contributions to the Social Security system would support 2.4 million American retirees.

- **The solvency of the Medicare trust fund would be extended if the undocumented population were able to gain legal status and citizenship.** Immigrants who are currently living in the United States without legal status could make a net contribution of $155 billion to Medicare over the next 30 years. Their contribution would extend the solvency of the Medicare trust fund by four years.

- **Passing the DREAM Act would inject billions of dollars into the American economy, while creating more than 1**

**million jobs.** The DREAM Act would provide a pathway to legal status for eligible young people who complete high school and some college or military service. At least $329 billion and 1.4 million jobs would be added to the American economy over the next two decades if the DREAM Act became law.

- **Expanding the Deferred Action program would immediately yield billions of dollars in tax revenues, while increasing wages and job security for all Americans.** Allowing low-priority unauthorized immigrants who have been in the country for five years to apply for deferred action—a temporary work permit and deferral of deportation—would mean that they could earn higher average wages and protection from exploitation. This would have a significant impact on the U.S. economy, yielding $6.1 billion in payroll tax revenue in the first year and increasing gains of up to $45 billion over the next five years.

## The record on immigrants and the economy

- **Undocumented immigrants pay billions of dollars in taxes annually.** Households headed by unauthorized immigrants paid $10.6 billion in state and local taxes in 2010. This includes $1.2 billion in personal income taxes, $1.2 billion in property taxes, and more than $8 billion in sales and excise taxes. Immigrants—even legal immigrants—are barred from most social services, meaning that they pay to support benefits they cannot even receive.
- **Research shows that immigrants complement, rather than compete with, native-born American workers—even less-skilled workers.** Research by renowned economists such as David Card, Gianmarco Ottaviano, Giovanni Peri, and Heidi Shierholz shows that American workers are not harmed by—and may even benefit from—immigration. This is because immigrants tend to complement the skillsets of American workers, thus helping them be more productive.

- **Immigration reform will not affect the unemployment rates of native-born Americans.** The CBO estimates that during the 10-year period following passage of immigration reform, unemployment will increase by 0.1 percent. This small increase falls entirely upon the undocumented and is the short-term effect of growth in the labor force and of the labor market adjusting to undocumented workers positioning themselves to be productive for decades to come.
- **Taxes paid by legalized immigrants more than offset any use of social programs.** The CBO found that increases in costs to social programs are modest and will be more than paid for by the tax contributions of immigrants. The increase in spending in Social Security and Medicare from 2024 through 2033, for example, will be $65 billion—just 4.4 percent of the total increase in tax revenue.
- **As Baby Boomers retire en masse over the next 20 years, immigrants will be crucial to fill these job openings and promote growth in the labor market.** More than two-thirds of new entrants into the labor market will replace retiring workers. However, while 58.6 million new workers will be needed to fill these retirements, only 51.3 million native-born people are projected to enter the workforce, meaning that immigrants and their children will be crucial to filling the additional 7.3 million job openings while also furthering growth in the labor market.

### The price of inaction and the cost of mass deportation

- **Inaction on immigration reform carries a heavy cost.** Each day the House of Representatives fails to pass immigration reform costs the United States $37 million in missed tax revenue. As of October 2014, the House's inaction has cost more than $17.7 billion.
- **Maintaining the status quo is not revenue neutral.** With only one-third of unauthorized immigrants working in the formal economy and contributing about $12 billion in payroll

taxes each year, the United States loses around $20 billion in payroll tax revenue annually. This lost revenue would go a long way toward funding the retirement of Americans across the country.

- **The United States spends more on immigration and border enforcement annually than the annual gross domestic product of 80 countries.** In fact, the United States now spends $3.5 billion more on immigration and border enforcement—a total of nearly $18 billion per year—than it does on all other federal law enforcement combined.
- **A self-deportation regime would cost our economy trillions of dollars.** If all undocumented immigrants in the country were deported or "self-deported"—meaning they choose to leave the country because life is too difficult—the United States' cumulative GDP would suffer a hit of $2.6 trillion over 10 years.
- **Mass deportation of the undocumented immigrant population would cost billions of dollars.** Deporting the entire undocumented population would cost $285 billion over a five-year period, including continued border and interior enforcement efforts. For that price, we could hire more than 1 million new public high school teachers and pay their salaries for five years.
- **It costs taxpayers more than $20,000 to carry out the deportation of a single individual.** Apprehending, detaining, processing, and transporting one individual in the deportation process cost $23,482 in fiscal year 2008.

[…]

# Periodical and Internet Sources Bibliography

*The following articles have been selected to supplement the diverse views presented in this chapter.*

George J. Borjas, "Yes, Immigration Hurts American Workers," *Politico*, September/October 2016. http://www.politico.com /magazine/story/2016/09/trump-clinton-immigration-economy -unemployment-jobs-214216.

Ben Casselman, "Immigrants Are Keeping America Young—And the Economy Growing," FiveThirtyEight, October 31, 2016. https:// fivethirtyeight.com/features/immigrants-are-keeping-america -young-and-the-economy-growing.

Michelle Chen, "Undocumented Immigrants Contribute Over $11 Billion to Our Economy Each Year," *Nation*, March 14, 2016. https://www.thenation.com/article/undocumented-immigrants -contribute-over-11-billion-to-our-economy-each-year.

Daniel Costa, David Cooper, and Heidi Shierholz, "Facts About Immigration and the U.S Economy," Economic Policy Institute, August 12, 2014. http://www.epi.org/publication/immigration -facts.

Adam Davidson, "Do Illegal Immigrants Actually Hurt the U.S Economy?" *New York Times*, February 12, 2013. http://www .nytimes.com/2013/02/17/magazine/do-illegal-immigrants -actually-hurt-the-us-economy.html.

Joseph P. DiNapoli and Kenneth B. Bleiwas, "The Role of Immigrants in the New York City Economy," Office of the New York State Comptroller, November 15, 2016. https://osc.state.ny.us/osdc /rpt7-2016.pdf.

Patrick Gillespie, "Immigration Economics: What You Need to Know," CNN Money, August 31, 2016. http://money.cnn .com/2016/08/31/news/economy/immigration-economics -trump-speech.

Gihoon Hong and John McLaren, "Are Immigrants a Shot in the Arm for the Local Economy?" National Bureau of Economic Research, April 2015. http://www.nber.org/papers/w21123.

Jeffrey Sparshot, "Immigration Does More Good Than Harm to the Economy, Study Finds," *Wall Street Journal*, September 22, 2016.

http://www.wsj.com/articles/immigration-does-more-good-than
-harm-to-economy-study-finds-1474568991.

John Ydstie, "Trump's Immigration Plan Could Undermine Promise
to Boost Economy," NPR, December 20, 2016. http://www.npr
.org/2016/12/20/505743200/trumps-immigration-plan-could
-undermine-promise-to-boost-economy.

# CHAPTER 4

# Do Increased Border Control and Deportations Actually Work?

# Chapter Preface

Beyond the debate over the effects of immigration on immigrants, US citizens, and the US economy and government, lies a narrower question: how can we enforce immigration laws? The answer has typically been a two-pronged approach: border control and deportations. While border control, most notably at the US-Mexico border, attempts to prevent migrants from entering into the United States in the first place or, at least, catching them as they do, deportations remove those who are already in the United States—and might have been for quite some time.

Internal immigration enforcement, or deportations, becomes notably tricky in some of these cases where families have resided together for years. As will be explored in this chapter, a particularly tragic (although not uncommon case) involves when two undocumented parents are deported, leaving young children with little to no support or oversight. Although deportations are an intensely debated topic, fewer people speak about what must be implemented in order to provide services for the children left behind. Recently, anti-immigration advocates have called for these children to be deported as well, whether or not they are legal US citizens. This call, however, is seen by many to ignore the right provided by the Fourteenth Amendment that "All persons born or naturalized in the United States, and subject to the jurisdiction thereof, are citizens of the United State and of the States wherein they reside."

Indeed, the debate on deportations forces us to think about the morality of separating families, among other issues. The question of efficiency must also arise. Some critics of forced deportations have argued that they are simply ineffective and that those who are deported will often enter back into the United States shortly thereafter, thus providing only economic strain and few real results. One of these critics, Alex Nowrasteh, convincingly argues that deportation does not successfully deter illegal immigration, but rather viable legal avenues to residency in the United States do. According to Nowrasteh and others, deportation might not only be ethically unsound but ineffective and costly as well. Rather, the US government should focus on increasing avenues for legal immigration, as it had done in the past with the Bracero program, for example. This has not quieted the cries for additional deportations and securitized walls to be built along the US-Mexico border, however, and the debate continues to rage.

> *"What Mr. Trump and other supporters of harsh enforcement actions like Operation Wetback won't tell you is that increased enforcement was combined with an increase in legal migration opportunities."*

# To Reduce Illegal Immigration, Allow Legal Immigration

*Alex Nowrasteh*

*In the following viewpoint, Alex Nowrasteh argues that an immigration enforcement plan implemented by the Eisenhower administration in the 1950s and used as a successful example by then-presidential candidate Donald Trump did not, by itself, reduce the amount of illegal immigration into the United States as some have argued. Rather, the immigration enforcement plan only worked in conjunction with the Bracero program, which allowed legal immigrants from Mexico into the United States temporarily for farm work. Nowrasteh suggests that any successful plan to reduce illegal immigration in the future must include avenues for legal immigration. Nowrasteh is an immigration policy analyst at the Center for Global Liberty and Prosperity of the Cato Institute and is an advocate for freer immigration into the United States.*

"Deportation Didn't End Illegal Migration in the '50s – Legal Immigration Did," by Alex Nowrasteh, Foundation for Economic Education, November 11, 2015. https://fee.org/articles/enforcement-didnt-end-illegal-immigration-in-the-50s-legal-immigration-did/. Licensed under CC BY 4.0 International.

As you read, consider the following questions:

1. According to the author, what reduced unauthorized immigration in the 1950s?
2. What does the author suggest future administrations can do to reduce illegal immigration while not relying on discriminatory or unethical practices?
3. What were some of the benefits and drawbacks of the Bracero program?

In last night's Republican presidential debate, Donald Trump argued that President Eisenhower's immigration enforcement plan, called "Operation Wetback" (Trump didn't use its horrendous name), drastically reduced unlawful immigration in the early 1950s. He said:

> Let me just tell you that Dwight Eisenhower. Good president. Great president. People liked him. I liked him. I Like Ike, right? The expression, "I like Ike." Moved 1.5 million illegal immigrants out of this country.
>
> Moved them just beyond the border, they came back. Moved them again beyond the border, they came back. Didn't like it. Moved 'em waaaay south, they never came back. Dwight Eisenhower. You don't get nicer, you don't get friendlier. They moved 1.5 million people out. We have no choice. We. Have. No. Choice.

The evidence and statements by border patrol and INS officials in the 1950s and afterward disagree with Mr. Trump's analysis.

Increased immigration enforcement did not reduce unauthorized immigration in the 1950s. Legal migration did.

## Background

In 1942, the United States government created the Bracero guest worker visa program to allow Mexican farm workers to temporarily work for American farmers during World War II. The government entered into a bilateral labor agreement with Mexico that regulated the migrant's wages, duration of employment, age of workers, health care, and transportation from Mexico to US farms.

Transportation to the farm, housing, and meals were sold by the employers for a low price. Ten percent of the migrant's wages were deducted from their paychecks and deposited in an account that would be turned over to them once they returned to Mexico.

The Bracero program did not limit the number of migratory workers as long as the government's conditions were met, making the system flexible to surges in demand. As a result, nearly five million Mexican workers used the Bracero program from its beginnings in 1942, when the first group of 500 braceros arrived at a farm in California, until the program's cancellation in 1964.

The program's flexibility increased over time as the Border Patrol and INS realized that the Bracero program was an indispensable component of reducing unlawful immigration by providing a lawful means of migration. During the early phase of the program, the United States government acted as the arbiter and distributor of the Mexican workers to American farms—heavily subsidizing the movement and not requiring total reimbursement for government expenses on medical and security screenings.

Later, as the number of unauthorized immigrants began to rise, the government reformed the program to allow for workers and employers to deal more directly with fewer regulations and government subsidies.

## Unauthorized Immigration in the 1950s

During the early, more regulated, and more restricted phase of the Bracero program, unauthorized immigrants continued to cross the border, which resulted in almost two million of them living in the United States by the early 1950s.

The immigration enforcement apparatus performed well when few unauthorized immigrants were trying to enter the Untied States during the Great Depression and World War II, but it suddenly broke down in the face of sustained postwar unlawful migration.

In 1946, the year after the war ended, an INS report recorded a massive increase in unauthorized entries that was "riddling the country of aliens illegally in the United States" with more illegal entries than any previous year. Reports in subsequent years reported the same steady increase in the number of illegal immigrants and enforcement actions (table 1).

In 1950-51, the volume of unauthorized Mexican immigrants was so high that the INS institutionalized a voluntary departure procedure that was quicker and cheaper than deportation. Government reports described the large increase in unauthorized immigration after World War II as "virtually an invasion."

**Table 1: Aliens Deported and Voluntary Departures, 1946-1952**

| YEAR | VOLUNTARY DEPARTURES | ALIENS DEPORTED |
|------|----------------------|-----------------|
| 1946 | 14,375 | 101,945 |
| 1947 | 18,663 | 195,880 |
| 1948 | 20,371 | 197,184 |
| 1949 | 20,040 | 276,297 |
| 1950 | 6,628 | 572,477 |
| 1951 | 13,544 | 673,169 |
| 1952 | 20,181 | 703,778 |

SOURCE: Congressional Research Service, 1980.

# Government Responses: Expanding Visas & Enforcement

The government responded to the increased illegal immigration with two interrelated and coordinated actions. The first and more important action (to say nothing of its humanity), was a legal reform and expansion of the Bracero guest worker visa program in 1951. The second was called "Operation Wetback," a nasty immigration enforcement operation begun in 1954 (it expanded from an earlier program) that removed almost two million unauthorized Mexicans in 1953-1954.

What Mr. Trump and other supporters of harsh enforcement actions like Operation Wetback won't tell you is that increased enforcement was combined with an increase in legal migration opportunities. Many of the migrants rounded up in the enforcement buildup to Operation Wetback were legalized on the spot—a long-standing process derogatively referred to as "drying out" illegal migrant workers—and given a Bracero work visa.

"Drying out" was not invented during Operation Wetback; it had been common practice beginning in 1947 and was made law in 1951. Although data is sparse on the number of unlawful migrants who underwent "drying out," 96,239 migrant workers were legalized in 1950 by that process, and the Department of Labor actually gave preference to legalizing unlawful migrants over admitting new Braceros.

Other unlawful migrants were driven down the border and made to take one step across the border and come back in as a legal Bracero worker, a process referred to as "a walk-around statute." The combination of a legal migration pathway with consequences for breaking immigration laws incentivized Mexican migrants to come legally.

As a result, the number of removals in 1955 was barely three percent of the previous year's numbers. Those who previously would have entered unlawfully instead signed up to become Braceros, which was the intended purpose of the reforms.

The government did not tolerate unlawful entry, but the INS made it very easy for migrants to get a guest worker visa and used the Border Patrol to funnel unauthorized migrants and potential unauthorized migrants into the legal system—sometimes simplifying the system beyond what Congress intended.

Increased lawful migration, flexibility, and enforcement funneled migrant workers into the Bracero program and reduced unauthorized immigration by an estimated 90 percent. The existence of a legal visa for lower skilled Mexican migrants was essential to the decrease in unlawful immigration.

## Bracero Deserved Credit for Halting Unauthorized Immigration, According to Border Patrol and INS

The Bracero program was effective at stopping unlawful immigration for two reasons.

First, it created a large and easy to use visa for farmers in the Untied States. If the cost of employing Bracero workers was too high, farmers would just hire unauthorized immigrants as they threatened to do numerous times—and Border Patrol and INS listened.

Prior to the expansion and partial deregulation of the Bracero program in 1951, employers in the Rio Grande Valley referred to the Border Patrol as a "Gestapo outfit" that wrenched their willing unlawful workers away from employment. Along with increased enforcement, INS Commissioner Joseph Swing realized that he would have to enlist the cooperation of the employers of unlawful migrant workers if the INS was to have any hope of shrinking the number of unauthorized workers. He knew he would have to affect both the supply and demand for unauthorized workers.

Before launching Operation Wetback, Swing traveled and spoke to numerous audiences and farmers assuring them that their unauthorized workers would be replaced with legal workers from Mexico on a Bracero work visa.

In Swing's words, the purpose of a ten-day trip to visit farmers along the border prior to the launch of Operation Wetback, was to tell them: "If there is any employer who cannot get legal labor all he has to do is let either the Department of Labor or Immigration know, and we will see that he gets it … I am quite emphatic about this because I know I am going to run into some opposition in Southern Texas."

Swing characterized the success as an "exchange" of illegal workers for legal guest workers. For example, the 1953 harvest in the Rio Grande Valley only employed 700 legal guest workers, while in 1954 the number had grown to 50,326. At every opportunity, Swing praised farmers and gave them credit for the substitution of illegal workers for legal Bracero workers, saying the "accomplishment of this task would have been impossible without the generous cooperation extended to the effort by ranchers, farmers, and growers."

Beginning in 1954, Commissioner Swing also issued I-100 cards to law-abiding Bracero workers who were favored by particular American growers, further simplifying the bureaucratic process for them to re-enter and work in the future. The INS eventually came to believe that the I-100 cards were an integral part of their efforts to keep unlawful immigration low.

The INS also made it easy for Braceros to move among farms to work, regardless of the original labor contract. As historian Ernesto Galarza wrote, "the most skeptical of farm employers could see that the private black market was no longer vital, now that a public one could be created at will."

The Bracero program made it economically advantageous for American employers of unlawful immigrants to cooperate with the Border Patrol and INS to ensure that their workforces were legal.

Second, the visa was also very easy for Mexican migrants to access and guaranteed that they would not have to work illegally and face the possibility of deportation. Over the course of the Bracero program, the INS and Border Patrol progressively removed the Mexican government from selecting the Bracero migrants and moved toward a model where US growers selected their workers—often based on previous experience with the individual migrant.

Removing the Mexican government from the process decreased opportunities for corruption and abuse of the workers. When the Mexican government was actively involved in selecting the Mexicans who could work in the United States prior to the reforms in 1951, the migrant often had to pay a mordida—a bribe—to Mexican officials. The migrant was then sent to a central processing center where he would have to pay yet another bribe to be considered.

The Mexican government was frustrated when the US government allowed American growers to unilaterally recruit Braceros, but cutting out the Mexican government middleman likely saved Braceros a lot of money and headaches.

From 1955 to 1960, annual bracero migration fluctuated between 400,000 and 450,000, and replaced the roughly two million unauthorized immigrants who moved to the United States after World War II. During this time, the government allowed braceros to work in virtually every sector of agriculture. The Bracero guest worker visa program, more so than any immigration enforcement system, practically eliminated unauthorized immigration.

A Border Patrol official warned that if the Bracero program was ever "repealed or a restriction placed on the number of braceros allowed to enter the United States, we can look forward to a large increase in the number of illegal alien entrants into the United States."

That official's prediction came true. When the Bracero program was ended in 1965 and not replaced by another effective lower skilled guest worker visa program, unlawful immigration as measured by the number of removals and returns skyrocketed (see Figure 1).

One legal worker on a visa seems to be worth more than one unauthorized immigrant worker—meaning a favorable trade off for those concerned about the number of guest workers who could migrate if a large guest worker program was implemented.

In 1954, one guest worker visa replaced 3.4 unauthorized immigrants, meaning that one legal worker seemed to be equal to more than three illegal workers (see Figure 1). That far fewer "physically able, adult male" Braceros could do the same quantity of work as several illegal workers was even noted at the time.

If an important goal of a lower skilled guest worker visa is to eliminate the American economic demand for unauthorized immigrants, relatively fewer guest worker visas can replace a much larger unauthorized immigrant population.

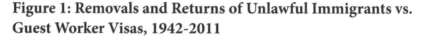

## Figure 1: Removals and Returns of Unlawful Immigrants vs. Guest Worker Visas, 1942-2011

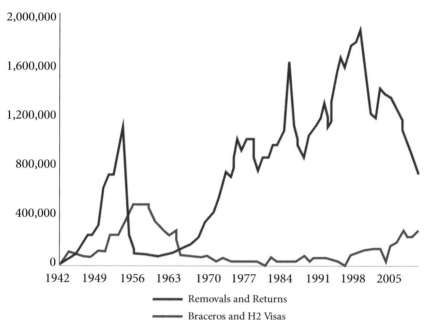

SOURCE: Department of Homeland Security and Immigration and Naturalization Service annual reports.

Figure 2 indicates that higher numbers of Border Patrol agents and increased border enforcement are unnecessary to get this result. When the government launched Operation Wetback and expanded the Bracero program, the number of border patrol agents did increase but only to a previous high.

By allowing unauthorized immigrants to get work visas, by not punishing them or employers for coming forward, and by making work visas available to future migrants, almost all future and current unauthorized immigrants can be funneled into the legal market without a large increase in enforcement. This was the policy followed in the 1950s, and it worked.

Clearly Operation Wetback should not be a guide for future enforcement policy because its racially discriminatory and harsh enforcement policies were unethical and legally unsound. However,

## Figure 2: Illegal Immigrants Removed and Returned vs. Border Patrol Agents, 1942-1960

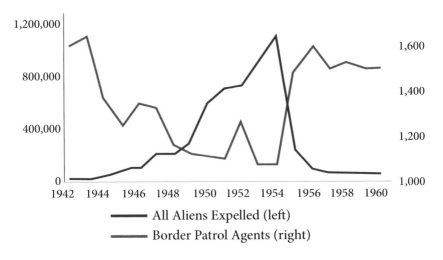

SOURCES: Department of Homeland Security, Immigration and Naturalization Service annual reports, and National Foundation for American Policy.

a new guest worker visa program combined with a refocused immigration enforcement system that seeks to channel unlawful and new migrants onto the guest worker visa could be effective.

## End of Bracero and Re-Ignition of Unlawful Immigration

By the time of Bracero's cancellation in 1964, increasing regulations promulgated by the Department of Labor (DoL) and restrictions whittled the number of Bracero guest worker visas down to just 200,000 that year. New DoL wage regulations and labor certification raised costs for farmers and migrants, incentivizing them to move into the informal, underground economy.

By making lawful employment of migrants so expensive, the government created unauthorized immigration. Since 1964, very few lower skilled workers have been allowed in, and the unauthorized immigrant population has skyrocketed. Ending

Bracero did not end temporary worker migration to the Untied States; it merely made such migration illegal.

After cancellation of the Bracero program, the H-2 guest worker visa became the source of legal foreign agricultural workers. The H-2 was underused relative to the Bracero program because of complex rules, numerical restrictions, and the cost of sponsoring migratory workers. The H-2 visa was initially created through the Immigration and Nationality Act of 1952 for "other temporary workers" not covered by the Bracero program. From 1964 until 1986, mostly temporary unauthorized Mexican migration filled the gap left by the repeal of the Bracero program, which was unfilled by the H-2 visa. After the end of Bracero, the modern age of unlawful immigration began as Figure 1 shows. The rest is history.

## Conclusion

Mr. Trump is correct that unauthorized immigration decreased markedly in the 1950s, but he is wrong to attribute all or even most of that to increased enforcement under the utterly inhumane "Operation Wetback." That operation would have been a complete failure if there was not a Bracero guest worker visa available to provide a legal avenue for lower skilled migration.

The Bracero program had a lot of problems, and any modern visa program would have to be very different, but it was better than the black market alternative. Border Patrol and INS agents at the time credited Bracero with ending unlawful immigration and predicted, correctly, that ending Bracero would reignite it.

Despite what Mr. Trump says, the lesson from the 1950s is not that harsh and inhumane immigration enforcement is effective, it is that a legal migration pathway can halt unlawful immigration.

> *"If some politicians and activists in the United States get their way, citizen children with two undocumented parents would have no choice but to return to their parent's country."*

# When Parents Get Deported, It's Their Children Who Suffer

*Erynn Elizabeth Reitmayer*

*In the following viewpoint, Erynn Elizabeth Reitmayer interviews a range of experts on immigration and families who have been affected by deportation, showing the traumatizing experiences many citizen children have when one or both of their undocumented parents are deported. When parents are deported, young children are often left to fend on their own without any supervision or aid from local governments. However, for some anti-immigration activists and politicians, their solution is that citizen children should be forcibly deported from the United States, as well, even if they have the "birthright" to stay on American soil. Reitmayer has a master's in journalism and mass communications from the Walter Cronkite School of Journalism.*

As you read, consider the following questions:

1. What do you think about the proposed plan to forcibly deport the citizen children of two undocumented parents from the United States?
2. What is the Birthright Citizenship Act?
3. How would you interpret the "jurisdiction" clause of the Fourteenth Amendment?

When the police arrived at his father's apartment, 1-year-old Christopher lay on the floor holding his 3-week-old brother. The boys were alone and covered in blood.

Christopher has vague memories of the event but says his mother and other relatives later described it to him in detail. He relies on memories and family stories as he recounts his early childhood.

Christopher was born in 1992 to a family of mixed immigration status. His father, a U.S. citizen, married his Mexican mother the year before his birth. Christopher says the relationship turned rocky because his father had a drug problem.

After the birth of her second son, Christopher's mother decided to leave her troubled husband for the benefit of her children; but when the husband found out what she planned to do, he threatened to call the police. Christopher says his father threatened to tell them his wife was not really the mother of their sons and have her deported so she could never take the children away.

"My mom was not afraid of him," Christopher said. "She said, 'Call them, and you'll see who your wife is.'"

His father wasn't bluffing.

He called the police. His Spanish-speaking wife had little recourse, unable to understand the scene that was unfolding. She was deported to Sinaloa, Mexico shortly thereafter, her two U.S. citizen sons left in the care of their citizen father.

"She was going crazy, in Mexico without us," Christopher said. "I was only 1 year and 7 months…my brother was just 3 weeks old."

Christopher said when his mother's best friend heard what had happened she went over to the apartment to talk to Christopher's father, but instead she found the two boys alone and Christopher injured. It appeared that Christoper had climbed into his brother's crib to comfort the crying boy. Lifting his brother out of the crib, he slipped, cutting his arm on the crib and falling to the floor.

"When they saw us like that, all covered in blood, everyone freaked out, wondering what was going on," Christopher said. "When they found my father, he was passed out on the street, on drugs and drunk. So they gave my mother a permit to come and get us, to take us back to Mexico."

[Repeated efforts to speak with Christopher's father for this story were unsuccessful.]

Christopher's story is not unique. According to a new study conducted by the Urban Institute, a research organization that focuses on social and economic issues, there are 5.5 million children that are currently living in the United States with at least one undocumented parent. Close to 75 percent of the children are U.S. citizens. When one or both parents are deported the result can be years of struggle for the citizen children. They often have to choose between living with their immediate family—in another country—or living without them in the United States. And, now, some conservatives are pushing legislation seeking to strip citizenship from children with two undocumented parents, meaning they would have no choice of which country to live in. The children would be deported along with their parents.

In the years following 1996's reforms to the Immigration and Nationality Act, efforts to detain and deport undocumented immigrants living illegally in the country have ramped up significantly. Workplace and residential raids have become a relatively common occurrence in some communities. This type of enforcement often leaves young citizens behind with little or no family support.

Margaret Acuitlapa faced a tough decision after her husband, an illegal immigrant, was deported. A U.S. citizen and mother of three, Acuitlapa had to decide whether to raise the children alone or uproot them and move to Mexico so they could be with their father. With her children's education in mind, Acuitlapa stayed in the United States for a month after her husband's deportation. However, she says the resulting emotional strain on the family proved overwhelming, and Acuitlapa decided to leave her home in Georgia to reunite her family in Mexico.

"The first year we were here, we were treated as strangers," Acuitlapa said of her family's arrival in Malinalco, a small town in southwestern Mexico. "Things were unpleasant for all of us."

Acuitlapa's family will have been living in the town three years as of this October—years she describes as very challenging.

"We have not been back home to visit once—and as you may have guessed, it is because of financial difficulties," Acuitlapa said.

Acuitlapa says that when she lived in the United States, her parents depended on her for rides to their many doctor's appointments. Her husband, Jose, would often help her father with strenuous jobs around the house, as he could no longer take care of everything on his own.

"They aren't in good health. So they can't even come visit us." Acuitlapa said. "We don't have the resources. I do feel trapped sometimes."

Although she moved to keep her family together, the life they have faced in Mexico has put different strains on her marriage, and her children.

"Our kids didn't speak any Spanish when we moved here. Even now, my 10-year-old daughter is reading at a second-grade level," she said of the struggles her children have faced in school. "My 15-year-old son is still having a hard time with everything."

Though she tries to keep in touch with her family back home, Acuitlapa says she has a hard time with being unable to see them.

"Tension has grown between my husband and I, and he blames himself that I'm depressed about missing my family," she said. "But I know things will work out. Because love does work."

## The Push to Undo Citizenship

Because Margaret and her children were citizens, they had a choice of which country to live in. If some politicians and activists in the United States get their way, citizen children with two undocumented parents would have no choice but to return their parent's country. They would be stripped of their citizenship and deported. Supporters of the concept often call citizen children of illegal immigrants "anchor babies," meaning they are an anchor that keeps illegal immigrants in the United States.

Former U.S. Rep. Nathan Deal, R-Ga., a leader among those targeting so-called "anchor babies," introduced Birthright Citizenship Act in 2009. The bill has 91 co-sponsors. (Until March of this year, Deal represented Georgia's 9th District. He has since resigned to make a run for governor of Georgia.)

The proposed legislation would amend the U.S. Immigration and Nationality Act so that children of illegal immigrants would not be considered citizens under the 14th Amendment to the Constitution, which grants citizenship for those born or naturalized in the United States and who are "subject to the jurisdiction thereof." The bill states that illegal immigrants and their children are not subject to the jurisdiction of the United States for the purpose of citizenship. The bill was sent to various U.S. House committees for consideration in 2009 but went no further.

One of the bill's well-known supporters is U.S. Rep. Brian Bilbray, a Republican who represents California's 50th district, which covers part of the greater San Diego area.

"The 14th Amendment of the Constitution has a conditioning clause: 'subject to the jurisdiction thereof,'" Bilbray said. "Undocumented immigrants, like tourists, are not subject to the jurisdiction of the United States; they aren't subject to the draft, you can't try them for treason."

Bilbray and other supporters of the legislation argue that it is constitutional. Under the Birthright Citizenship Act, any child born within the U.S. who has at least one citizen parent, a parent who is a legal permanent resident or a parent serving in the military would still be granted citizenship.

Therefore, Bilbray contends, if a parent is subject in one of these ways to the jurisdiction of the government, then the child could rightfully be considered a citizen.

Bilbray says that citizenship is a right that must be earned.

"It isn't the soil or the climate," Bilbray said. "It's the parent, through their obligation to the government, that earn their children citizenship."

Kevin Johnson, the dean and professor of law at the University of California, Davis, disagrees. He says Bilbray and others are misinterpreting the "jurisdiction" clause in the 14th Amendment.

"That language was designed to deal with the children of foreign diplomats, who are immune from suit and the laws of the United States while in the United States," he says. "If proponents of this idea were correct, that would mean undocumented immigrants are not subject to the civil and criminal laws of a state and could not be sentenced to prison for crimes."

Lino Graglia, a law professor at the University of Texas, supports the idea of revoking the citizenship of children with illegal immigrant parents, arguing that automatic citizenship creates an incentive to break the law.

"It doesn't really make sense," Graglia says. "If you're going to prohibit something, why create a powerful inducement to do it? We make it illegal to come into the country without permission, but if you do it anyway and have children your children are rewarded with citizenship. It's contrary."

Graglia says it does not matter that children who have spent their entire lives in the United States may suddenly find themselves deported to a completely unfamiliar environment, where they don't speak the language or understand the culture.

"Their parents broke the law and came to the country illegally," Graglia says. "Just as their parents are, they should be subject to deportation."

Hiroshi Motomura, a professor at the UCLA School of Law has the opposite opinion.

"These children are innocent, even if conceding their parents culpability, so we shouldn't penalize them," Motomura says. "Regardless of how they got here, the law should recognize the ties developed and contributions made in this country—especially economically—by unauthorized migrants and their families."

Other lawmakers are urging reform that would help protect citizen children of undocumented immigrants. U.S. Rep. Jose E. Serrano, D-N.Y., introduced the Child Citizen Protection Act in 2006; the act would amend the immigration reforms of 1996 such that judges would have discretion to consider the best interests of children in deportation hearings. Deportation would not be a forgone conclusion.

## Born in the Air?

Kendrick Nunez, 18, is one of those citizen children who would be affected if the "anchor baby" bill became law. He and his citizen sister currently live in Arkansas without their parents, who were deported to Mexico. He finds the logic of the movement confusing.

"That seems unreasonable. What, you're just born in the air?" Nunez says. "I recognize there is a problem, but there has to be a better solution."

Nunez and his younger sister initially followed their parents and other siblings to Mexico but returned to the United States so they could continue studying within the American education system.

"I didn't go to school when I was in Mexico. I spent my time working—in a car wash, a water park, a field," Nunez said. "I was illegal there. All my best friends in Arkansas were graduating. I felt like I was missing out on something."

## Returning Home

Hope for an education brought Christopher back into the United States nearly 13 years after his departure. As a teenager growing up in Mexico, Christopher would often daydream about the future he could have in America and the possibilities that might await him if he returned.

"We were home-schooled through elementary, and my mother was very protective," Christopher recalls of the years he spent in Sinaloa with his mother. "I always wanted to be doing what the other kids were doing."

When he finished elementary school, Christopher begged his mother to place him in a public school so he could experience more than the small world he knew living in their small home. She enrolled him in, and he started in the fall.

"I was shocked at seeing so many kids!" Christopher said. "They all called me a nerd because I was studious, and I was better educated from being home-schooled."

Christopher said there were 56 students to a room—a hard adjustment for someone who had constant attention while being home-schooled.

It wasn't long before his dreams once again outgrew his circumstances.

"I started thinking, 'What am I going to be, what kind of man am I going to become?'" Christopher said. "At the same time, I was realizing how exciting I found America to be."

Part of Christopher's extended family resides in Texas, and he describes visiting as a young teenager and being in awe of his home country.

"Seeing the United States was like a dream," he said. "Everything was so perfect. I was amazed. I told my mother, one day I wanted to come to the United States and study English so I can live my life here."

Christopher says his mother agreed that he should return to the United States and take advantage of the future available to him as a citizen, but she hadn't expected that he would make the decision to go by himself at the age of fourteen.

"A dream was placed in my mind," Christopher said. "I knew that the goal would be difficult for me, but I was motivated to make this change."

Christopher returned to America to as a bright-eyed teenager, intent on making the most of the opportunities he would not have in Mexico. He didn't realize that what lay ahead were years of struggle.

## Parents Deported, Children in Foster Care

Because Christopher's only legal parent, his citizen father, was unable to be his guardian, he accompanied his mother back to Mexico as a young child. When a citizen child is left in this situation—either because both parents are deported or a legal parent is unable to take custody—they often end up staying with relatives who have legal status, entering public foster care or wandering homeless. Complications surrounding a parent's ability to come to the United States after they have been deported can make it difficult, or impossible, for some deported parents to regain their parental rights, meaning that their children can be put in foster care for long periods of time or put up for adoption.

Such was the case for Nathaly Perez's mother, who was deported in June 2008, leaving her three teenage daughters behind.

Perez, now 18, was born in San Diego to a large family with varying immigration status. Her parents and four older siblings were all born in Mexico. Nathaly's sister Eralia, now 19, was just over a year old when the Perez family moved the to the United States. Her two older brothers and eldest sister were nearly grown. Over the next two years, her mother had Nathaly and another daughter.

Although Perez's father immigrated legally, his status was revoked when he and Perez's mother were both jailed for a domestic disturbance. He was subsequently deported in 2006. Perez's mother was given probation. Following her father's deportation, Perez recalls her mother struggling to support the family alone, sometimes working two or more jobs to care for her three young daughters.

Eralia Perez points to her father's sudden, complete absence as the catalyst for a pattern of unhealthy behavior that would continue for years to come.

"I was only 14 years old when he was deported. Everything changed," Perez said. "I started making bad choices. I wouldn't listen to my mom."

Eventually, the Perez sisters would also have to deal with losing their mother. Two years after their father's deportation their eldest sister filed a report alleging that the girls' older brothers were abusive towards their youngest sister. As the boys both had prior records, they were not legally allowed to be living with their mother, because probationers can only live together if they have court permission.

"Before this happened, my mom had been doing really well. She was doing awesome," Nathaly recalls. "I don't know if anything was going on with my brothers. We didn't know about it. "

Perez's mother and two older brothers were arrested and deported in the following months, and all three girls were placed in public foster care.

After losing so many close family members, Nathaly says she struggled to find stability.

"Little by little I felt like everybody was getting taken away from me. To me, in my head, I was just ready for my sister Eralia to be deported," Nathaly said.

## Inspiration from a Foster Parent

Eralia, also an undocumented immigrant, had been struggling for some time before her mother's deportation, and it took her several years to get back on solid ground. During that time, she was separated from her younger sisters and sent to live in a different home in the small, rural town of Jackson, Calif.

"The part that killed me the most was that when I finally wanted to stop doing all that running around and come home and make up for that lost time with my mom, it was too late," Eralia said.

In time, Eralia finally found a foster mother who helped her realize who she wanted to be and gave her the structure and stability she needed to get there. She recently graduated from high school and received her green card.

Nathaly also graduated this past June, and looks forward to attending college in the future.

"I don't know for sure what I'm going to do yet," she says. "I just know I'm going to do my best, and keep striving."

The Perez sisters were able to find foster parents that not only made them feel loved but provided them with role models they could respect. That is not the case for many children who are placed in the system.

Hemal Sharifzada is a former foster youth who now works for California Youth Connection, an organization that advocates for foster care support and educates foster youth on how they can navigate the world of adulthood when they may not have family support.

Sharifzada says that one of the biggest hurdles many foster youth will face is trying to find a place where they feel loved and supported.

"You build a lot of barriers. Everyone is kind of a question mark," he says, speaking from years of experience. "You're always thinking, 'Who are you, how long are you going to be around—are you going to leave, are you going to stay? Does it matter?'"

Sharifzada says that the trust issues and emotional struggles common among foster youth often carry into adulthood and can complicate future relationships.

There are no nationwide statistics on the number of citizen children placed in foster care after a parent's deportation.

But according to numbers reported by the Department of Health and Human Services, if 10 percent of the approximately 5 million children of undocumented parents were placed in foster care, this would double the number of children in the system, which is already overburdened. In 2009 by the Child Welfare League of America reported the cost for public foster care exceeds $4 billion per year.

Financial estimates don't take into account the human costs of placing a child in foster care. According to the report by the

Child Welfare League of America, an estimated 85 percent of all youth in public foster care have an emotional disorder, a substance abuse problem or both. Statistics indicate that children who grow up in foster care will experience a wide variety of hardships at a much higher rate than the general population.

## Homeless, Hungry, and Wandering

Not all children of deported parents will end up in foster care, but even those who don't often lack basic family support.

Stephen Coger, a social worker in Arkansas, has worked with many undocumented immigrants in his town of Fayetteville. Coger says that even the loss of one parent tends to have an extremely negative effect on the upbringing of a child.

"Food hardship is one of the most common occurrences for children in these situations," Coger says. "Often these families need both incomes. When a parent is deported the household income decreases significantly."

Homelessness can also become a consequence. When Christopher returned to America, he found friends and family members in Arizona willing to take him in—but only for a time.

In many ways, he lived like most American teenagers. He attended high school and played tennis on the school team. Having always been a creative child, he found the arts especially stimulating.

"It was really hard at first because I didn't speak English. My mom thought that after a month I would give up," he said, laughing. "She was amazed how well I did after only a semester. She said she was really proud of me."

But Christopher struggled trying to find a place within families that weren't his own. One night, after his presence caused a bitter argument among relatives who had taken him in, he ran away. After spending a terrifying night alone in a park, he was able to find a friend's family willing to take him in.

The family lived close to some of Christopher's other relatives. The mother of the family remembers her son's friend as being isolated from family.

"I know he sometimes talked to his grandmother and aunt in California … and of course his mother. But his father didn't seem to be in the picture," she said. "He didn't really have anyone to depend on."

Unfortunately, things didn't get easier from there; in just a few months, the economic downturn resulted in his friend's father losing his job.

"It was some of the best times of my life, living with that family," Christopher says. "When they told me they couldn't afford to have me anymore, I told them it was OK. I told them that they had saved my life."

At the age of 15, Christopher found himself cleaning his community church to earn room and board there. In time, he found another family willing to take him in.

"I was glad to have a place to live, but I was doing a lot of work around the house to earn my keep," he said. "That was my junior year. It was hard for me to see all the other kids having fun, being kids."

In spite of these struggles, Christopher says he never regretted his decision to return to the United States. Instead of seeing a country that has let him down, he sees the country of the American Dream—a dream that as a citizen he is entitled to.

## Education & the American Dream

The desire to help immigrants take part in the American Dream drove Jose "Joe" Kennard to take action. A successful real estate investor and land developer, Kennard founded the Organization to Help Citizen Children with hopes that he might find like-minded community members to spark a movement toward providing better options for citizen children.

Until two years ago, Kennard and his wife lived in Seattle—as did Ana Reyes, a woman Kennard had never met. Unlike Kennard, however, Reyes was living and working in the country illegally. In 2007, U.S. immigration officials came to arrest Reyes early on the morning of her birthday. It was also the day her 13-year-old daughter Julie Quiroz was to graduate from seventh grade. Instead, Quiroz spent the afternoon helping her grandmother empty her family's Seattle home, preparing herself and her younger sister to move to Mexico.

"I just remember looking out the window and seeing my mom in handcuffs," Quiroz says. "My little sister was crying. Then we had to empty out the house … It kind of felt like this was it."

Shortly after, Quiroz was reunited with her mother, brother and stepfather—in Mexico. The whole family had been deported. She began attending school, but was soon frustrated by her inability to keep up.

"I couldn't read or write Spanish! I felt out of place, like I didn't belong," she said. "I only went to school for two weeks … then I guess I just gave up. I couldn't understand anything."

After she dropped out of school, help came to Quiroz's family in an unexpected way. Having read an article about her family's plight in The Seattle Times one Sunday, Joe Kennard felt compelled to help Julie—and all citizen children placed in these situations.

"I read the follow-up article about what was happening with Julie since her family was deported. I found the article really heart wrenching," Kennard remembers. "I couldn't shake it. We went to church and continued our usual routine, but when we got home I told my wife about it. I told her I felt like maybe the Lord was calling me to help this family."

Kennard says his wife was supportive of what he felt he had to do.

"She just says, 'If that's what you think he's telling you, then that's what you ought to do,'" Kennard said.

Kennard began communicating by phone with Ana Reyes, trying to think of a solution for her daughter Julie and other kids in her situation.

"I did some research, and I thought that the best way to help would be to get churches involved," Kennard says. "I thought if we could get a network of families started through churches on both sides of the border we could create a support system for the children to go back and forth."

Kennard provided funding for Reyes to move from Mexico City to Juarez so that Julie could attend school across the border in El Paso. He arranged for a family to take Julie in during the school week, and she would return to her mother on weekends.

"The idea was to minimize the trauma on these children by finding legal alternatives," Kennard says of his idea.

In time, the violence in Juarez became a concern for Reyes, and she worried for the safety of herself and her two young daughters. She decided to move back to Mexico City. Kennard, who was committed to helping Julie achieve her dreams, extended her the offer of taking up residence with himself and his family for the entire school year.

"I had to make the choice to go with my mom in Mexico or stay here with the Kennards," Quiroz says. "It was a really hard choice, but I decided to stay."

Kennard and his wife returned to his native Texas. He opened an authentic Mexican restaurant that serves his mother's traditional dishes in the downtown square and continues to advocate for the rights of citizen children.

"The problem is that we are punishing the children, and they are innocents in this situation," Kennard says. "The laws aren't protecting them—and as citizens they deserve to have their rights taken into consideration."

According to a 2009 study by Human Rights Watch, nearly every major human rights treaty recognizes the need for special protection of children. The United Nations Convention on the Rights of the Child, for example, explicitly states that every child has the right to know and be cared for by his or her parents.

Though Kennard is glad to be doing his part to find a solution, he says he has been disheartened that his organization hasn't gotten much traction.

"What was really surprising to me was that we couldn't really get churches to help," Kennard says. "To me, at the time, fellow evangelicals weren't acting very Christian. They were saying that these people were illegal, and obeying the law is a biblical mandate …. To me, the overriding biblical mandate is 'Love your neighbor.' I couldn't believe fellow Christians were taking such a cavalier-or sometimes outright hostile- attitude toward these families."

But luckily for Julie Quiroz, now 15, Joe Kennard stepped up to become the defender of her rights. Quiroz currently lives with Kennard and his family at their home in Waxahachie, Texas. She attends a local school, where she is excelling, but the opportunity comes with a downside. She only sees her family on Christmas and summer vacation, when she travels to Mexico for the school break.

"It's hard, always having to leave them again," Quiroz says. "It's like I almost don't want to get very attached to them, because I know I have to go—but of course it's hard not to get attached."

Quiroz knows she is lucky. Many children in her situation may see their families even less, if at all. Kendrick Nunez hasn't seen his family in more than six months; the Perez sisters haven't seen their mother since she was deported more than two years ago. In spite of the obstacles that have been placed in front of these children, each of them has expressed a desire to remain in the United States.

"I don't know what I'd be doing if I stayed there [in Mexico]," Quiroz says. "Probably doing nothing with my life, making nothing of myself."

For Christopher, the future is getting brighter—but his achievements have been hard won with years of difficulty and uncertainty. He was able to find a home at the Tumbleweeds Center for Youth Development in Phoenix and was accepted to Arizona State University for the coming fall. He puts his creativity to good use, participating in Phoenix's popular art walk on the first Friday of every month.

"I am glad that I came here, even if I had to go through those hard times," he says. "It's made me who I am."

> *"Securing the U.S.-Mexico border—*
> *with an electronic fence, which has*
> *worked so effectively in Israel—is*
> *more urgent than we think."*

# Securing the Mexican Border Will Protect the US from ISIS

*Raymond Ibrahim*

*In the following viewpoint, Raymond Ibrahim writes about the necessity of building a securitized wall along the US-Mexico border due to the fact that ISIS fighters are crossing into the United States from Mexico. He bases his argument on the "undisputed" fact that ISIS fighters have built bases of operations in Mexico in order to enter into the United States and carry out attacks. However, Ibrahim only relies on information from partisan and potentially unreliable sources. In fact, many of these claims have been debunked; in June 2015, the State Department wrote, "There were no known international terrorist organizations operating in Mexico … [and] no evidence that any terrorist group has targeted US citizens in Mexican territory." Ibrahim is a widely published author, public speaker, and Middle East and Islam specialist whose writings have appeared in the* New York Times, *on CNN, on Fox News, and in the* Financial Times.

As you read, consider the following questions:

1.  What are some of the practical difficulties of building a wall along the US-Mexico border that are not mentioned here?
2.  Is the information included as evidence convincing or not?
3.  Do you think the evidence presented proves the three "undisputed" facts included here?

- If you really want to protect Americans from ISIS, you secure the southern border. It's that simple."—Rep. Duncan Hunter.
- The Department of Homeland Security denied Hunter's claims, called them "categorically false" and added that "no credible intelligence to suggest terrorist organizations are actively plotting to cross the southwest border." Days later, however, it was confirmed that "4 ISIS Terrorists" were arrested crossing the border into Texas.
- Under Obama's presidency alone, 2.5 million illegals have crossed the border. And those are just the ones we know about. How many of these are ISIS operatives, sympathizers or facilitators?
- Securing the U.S.-Mexico border—with an electronic fence, which has worked so effectively in Israel—is more urgent than we think.

O f all the reasons a majority of Americans support the plan of businessman and U.S. presidential candidate Donald Trump to "build a wall" along the U.S.-Mexico border, perhaps the most critical is to avoid letting terrorists into the country. Drugs enter, the victims of traffickers enter, but the most imminent danger comes from operatives of the Islamic State (ISIS) and like-minded groups that are trying to use this porous border as a way to smuggle weapons of mass destruction (WMDs) into the United States and launch terror attacks that could make 9/11 seem like a morning in May. Just last week, "One of the American men accused in Minnesota of trying to join the Islamic State group wanted to open up routes from Syria to the U.S. through Mexico... Guled Ali Omar told the ISIS members about the route so that it could be used to send members to America to carry out terrorist attacks, prosecutors alleged in a document."

ISIS, however, did not need to be "told" by Ali "about the route." Nearly a year earlier, ISIS explored options on how it could smuggle a WMD "into the U.S. through Mexico by using existing trafficking networks in Latin America."

The Islamic State's magazine *Dabiq* last May (issue #9) published the following scenario:

> Let me throw a hypothetical operation onto the table. The Islamic State has billions of dollars in the bank, so they call on their wilāyah [province] in Pakistan to purchase a nuclear device through weapons dealers with links to corrupt officials in the region. ... The weapon is then transported over land until it makes it to Libya, where the mujāhidīn [jihadis] move it south to Nigeria. Drug shipments from Columbia bound for Europe pass through West Africa, so moving other types of contraband from East to West is just as possible. The nuke and accompanying mujāhidīn arrive on the shorelines of South America and are transported through the porous borders of Central America before arriving in Mexico and up to the border with the United States. From there it's just a quick hop through a smuggling tunnel and hey presto, they're mingling with another 12 million "illegal" aliens in America with a nuclear bomb in the trunk of their car.

The ISIS publication added that if not a nuke, "a few thousand tons of ammonium nitrate explosive," which is easily manufactured, could be smuggled.

Such thinking is hardly new. Back in 2009, a Kuwaiti cleric explained how easy it would be to murder countless Americans by crossing through the Mexican border:

Four pounds of anthrax—in a suitcase this big—carried by a fighter through tunnels from Mexico into the U.S. are guaranteed to kill 330,000 Americans within a single hour if it is properly spread in population centers there. What a horrifying idea; 9/11 will be small change in comparison. Am I right? There is no need for airplanes, conspiracies, timings and so on. One person, with the courage to carry 4 pounds of anthrax, will go to the White House lawn, and will spread this "confetti" all over them, and then we'll do these cries of joy. It will turn into a real celebration.

Plans aside, ISIS and other Islamic terrorists are based in and coming from Mexico. The evidence is piling up. In August 2014, Judicial Watch reported that ISIS was "operating in the Mexican border city of Ciudad Juarez and planning to attack the United States with car bombs or other vehicle borne improvised explosive devices." Months later in April 2015, ISIS was exposed operating in the northern Mexican state of Chihuahua—eight miles from the U.S.

In October 2014, Rep. Duncan Hunter (R-Calif) said, "I know that at least 10 ISIS fighters have been caught coming across the Mexican border in Texas." The Department of Homeland Security (DHS) emphatically denied Hunter's claims, called them "categorically false" and added that "no credible intelligence to suggest terrorist organizations are actively plotting to cross the southwest border." Days later, however, it was confirmed that "4 ISIS Terrorists" were arrested crossing the border into Texas.

On September 20, 2015, "U.S. Border Patrol nabbed two Pakistani men with ties to terrorism at the U.S.-Mexico border. … Both men … took advantage of smuggling networks or other routes increasingly used by Central American illegal immigrants to sneak into the U.S."

This is uncomfortably reminiscent of the scenario outlined in the ISIS magazine: after naming Pakistan as the nation from which to acquire nukes—the two men arrested for "ties to terrorism" were from Pakistan—the *Dabiq* excerpt explained: "The nuke and accompanying mujāhidīn... are transported through the porous borders of Central America before arriving in Mexico and up to the border with the United States. From there it's just a quick hop through a smuggling tunnel."

On December 2, 2015, "A Middle Eastern woman was caught surveilling a U.S. port of entry on the Mexican border holding a sketchbook with Arabic writing and drawings of the facility and its security system." Around the same time, "five young Middle Eastern men were apprehended by the U.S. Border Patrol in Amado, an Arizona town situated about 30 miles from the Mexican border. Two of the men were carrying stainless steel cylinders in backpacks..."

These arrests clearly indicate that Islamic terrorists are crossing the border into the U.S. For every illegal person caught, how many are not? One estimate says that at best only half of those illegally crossing the border are ever apprehended. Under Obama's presidency alone, 2.5 million illegals have crossed the border. And those are just the ones we know about. How many of these are ISIS operatives, sympathizers or facilitators? Border guards cannot even be "especially alert" for terrorists: many easily blend in with native Mexicans.

Three facts are undisputed: 1) ISIS and other terrorist groups see Mexico as a launching pad for terrorist acts in the U.S.; 2) ISIS and other terrorist groups have bases of operations in Mexico; 3) Members of ISIS and other terrorist groups have been caught trying to enter through the border.

In other words, it is just a matter of time. As Rep. Duncan Hunter once put it:

> If you really want to protect Americans from ISIS, you secure the southern border. It's that simple. ISIS doesn't have a navy, they don't have an air force, they don't have nuclear weapons. The only way that ISIS is going to harm Americans is by coming in through the southern border—which they already have.

Just as before 9/11—when U.S. leadership had received ample warnings of a spectacular terrorist attack targeting the U.S.—this problem may well be ignored until a spectacular attack occurs: San Bernardino was apparently too small, it did not count. Then, it will be more of the usual from the comatose media and many politicians: "shock," handwringing, and appeals against "Islamophobia."

Securing the U.S.-Mexico border—with an electronic fence, which has worked so effectively in Israel—is more urgent than we think.

> "Interior enforcement is only part
> of the government's immigration
> enforcement strategy and must
> also be looked at as a component of
> broader immigration enforcement
> that includes border enforcement."

# Border Security Is the Most Effective Way to Control Immigration

*Alex Nowrasteh*

*In the following viewpoint, Alex Nowrasteh argues that deportation and border security should not be seen as complements that work together to decrease immigration, but as substitutes for one another. According to Nowrasteh, border security is the most effective and efficient way of controlling immigration, instead of forced deportations, and has been done to great effect by the Obama administration—despite the criticisms of some anti-immigration groups. However, Nowrasteh is an advocate for freer immigration and believes that legal pathways for immigrants are an integral part of enforced and fair immigration laws. Nowrasteh is an immigration policy analyst at the Center for Global Liberty and Prosperity of the Cato Institute and is an advocate for freer immigration into the United States.*

"Obama's Deportation Numbers: Border and Interior Immigration Enforcement Are Substitutes, Not Complements," by Alex Nowrasteh, Cato Institute, March 31, 2014. http://www.cato.org/blog/obamas-deportation-numbers-border-interior-immigration-enforcement-are-substitutes-not. Licensed under CC BY 3.0.

As you read, consider the following questions:

1. What is the difference between interior enforcement, or deportations, and border enforcement? How did the Obama administration address both of these components of immigration enforcement, according to the author?

2. According to Nowrasteh, border control has become more efficient in recent years. Why?

3. According to the author, what is the best way to have well-enforced immigration laws?

It's become clear over the last few months that something very funny is going on with immigration enforcement statistics. The data generally show that interior enforcement, what most people commonly think of as "deportations" (but also includes I-9, Secure Communities, and E-Verify), has declined as a percentage of total removals. Many of the removals appear to be unlawful immigrants apprehended by Customs and Border Protection (CBP) and then turned over to Immigration and Customs Enforcement (ICE) for removal – a trend that began in 2012 and accelerated in 2013. That transfer makes it appear as if there was more internal enforcement than there really was. The administration is therefore deporting an increasing number of recent border crossers and a decreasing number of unlawful immigrants apprehended in the interior.

It appears, then, that President Obama's reputation for severe interior enforcement was earned for 2009, 2010, and 2011 but is somewhat unjustified in 2012 and 2013. The Bipartisan Policy Center has an excellent report on the enormous court backlogs and other issues that have arisen due to interior immigration enforcement. I'm waiting for additional information from a FOIA request before wading into the data surrounding the interior versus border removals controversy because we do not have data on internal enforcement numbers prior to 2008.

Interior enforcement is only part of the government's immigration enforcement strategy and must also be looked at as a component of broader immigration enforcement that includes border enforcement.

Jessica Vaughan at the Center for Immigration Studies (CIS) combines returns at the border and removals that appears to show President Obama as the weakest immigration enforcer in decades. Her conclusion mistakenly conflates lower numbers of unauthorized immigrant crossers with a lack of enforcement. Since fewer unauthorized immigrants are crossing the border now than prior to the Great Recession, the decrease in returns is due to the decreasing quantity of crossers and not a lack of enforcement. However, Vaughan's combination of border enforcement's returns of unlawful immigrants and interior enforcement's deportation numbers rightly shows how linked these two functions of immigration enforcement are.

After reading research from CIS for years, I can safely assume that they view border and interior immigration enforcement as complementary. Increased border enforcement multiplies the effectiveness of interior enforcement and vice versa. Under their view, less interior enforcement will lead to less effective immigration enforcement even if all of those resources are transferred to border enforcement—losing out on the supposed synergies that only exist when both types of enforcement work in tandem. Unsurprisingly, I think interior and border enforcement are more likely to be substitutes than complements—but imperfect substitutes. Moreover, many more resources would have to be devoted to interior enforcement to get the same deterrent effect from an equivalent amount of resources devoted toward border enforcement.

Some history of immigration enforcement strategy: Since the mid-1990s, the border enforcement strategy has been one of "prevention through deterrence"—the idea that concentrating personnel, infrastructure, and surveillance along the most crossed regions of the border will most effectively discourage unlawful immigration. By reducing the flow, the long run gradual attrition and voluntary return migration will gradually reduce the stock of unauthorized immigrants.

According to the Congressional Research Service,

> [s]ince 2005, CBP has attempted to discourage repeat entries and disrupt migrant smuggling networks by imposing tougher penalties against certain unauthorized aliens, a set of policies eventually described as "enforcement with consequences." Most people apprehended at the Southwest border are now subject to "high consequence" enforcement outcomes. Across a variety of indicators, the United States has substantially expanded border enforcement resources over the last three decades. Particularly since 2001, such increases include border security appropriations, personnel, fencing and infrastructure, and surveillance technology.

The strategic goals of interior enforcement are similar to the goals of border enforcement. According to Bryan Roberts, Ted Alden, and John Whitley at the Council on Foreign Relations, the goals of interior enforcement are to "turn off the jobs magnet" and prompt "attrition through enforcement" (pp. 34-35). In other words, the strategic goal of interior immigration enforcement is to deter the entry of unauthorized immigration and then incentivize the return of those who come anyway.

This leads us to the issue of whether interior enforcement is even effective.

Assuming that the effectiveness of immigration enforcement should be maximized, shifting immigration enforcement actions from interior to border enforcement makes more sense. Bryan Roberts, Ted Alden, and John Whitley sum up the studies and evidence comparing the marginal effectiveness of additional resources spent on border versus interior enforcement (pp. 34-38). For both categories, the main effect is to change immigrant behavior once in the United States or to change their mode of entry. The decision to unlawfully enter is not reconsidered due to increased internal enforcement. The exceptions are two studies that purported to find that increased interior enforcement was

## OBAMA'S HIGH DEPORTATION RATE

In an interview with Telemundo's Jose Diaz-Balart on Tuesday, President Obama said that it would be difficult to halt the deportation of immigrants living in the country illegally without the approval of Congress.

Immigration rights advocates have pushed the president to halt deportations through an executive order, especially of immigrants who haven't committed any serious crimes.

Last summer the administration did just this for young unauthorized immigrants brought to the country illegally as children with the creation of the "Deferred Action for Childhood Arrivals" program. Known as DREAMers, more than 500,000 young unauthorized immigrants have taken advantage of the administration's program. Our 2012 survey of Hispanic adults found wide approval (89% approved of this new policy). A Pew Research Center survey of the general U.S. public found that 63% of U.S. adults approved of this program as well.

But deportations of unauthorized immigrants continue at record levels. In 2011 some 392,000 immigrants were removed from the U.S., according to the Department of Homeland Security. Among them, 48% were deported for breaking U.S. laws, such as drug trafficking, driving under the influence and entering the country illegally.

The Obama Administration has deported more immigrants annually than the George W. Bush Administration.

**"High Rate of Deportations Continue Under Obama Despite Latino Disapproval," by Mark Hugo Lopez and Ana Gonzalez-Barrera, Pew Research Center, September 19, 2013.**

twice as cost effective as border enforcement in Arizona, mainly by lowering the wage for unauthorized immigrants. Those studies were written before it was revealed how ineffective E-Verify has been in lowering wages for unauthorized immigrants in Arizona (the results might be different if E-Verify was nationalized), so the deterrent effect is likely less than reported.

The counter argument to the common finding that interior enforcement is inefficient is that it has not really been tried, so we don't necessarily know how effective it could be if more resources were devoted to it. Given the disappointing (from the restrictionist point of view) results of E-Verify, the lack of studies investigating the deterrent effect of Secure Communities, and the known effectiveness of border enforcement in deterring unlawful entries, shifting resources from internal enforcement to border enforcement is likely a better use of scarce resources to disincentivize unauthorized immigration.

Border enforcement is likely getting more effective. A December 2012 GAO report found that about 81 percent of all those who attempted to enter illegally along the Southwest border in 2011 were either apprehended or turned back (caution, the denominator is not always known here). That percentage is up dramatically from previous years.

## Get Aways, Apprehensions, Turnbacks, and Estimated Getaways

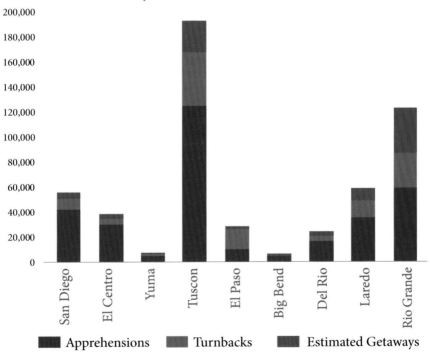

SOURCE: GAO

## Apprehensions and Turnbacks as a Percent of Estimated Unlawful Entries

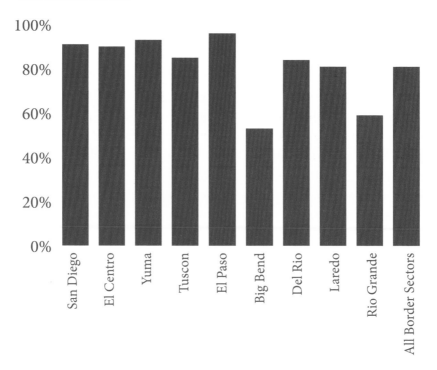

SOURCE: GAO

The government has been getting better at border security although the decrease in the number of unauthorized border crossers due to the poor economy can take most of the credit. The reallocation of interior immigration enforcement resources to border enforcement appears to be rational from the perspective of a government seeking to increase the deterrent effect of immigration enforcement. Effective border security likely affects the flow of unauthorized immigrants more directly than the stock, but it also leads to long run decreases in the latter.

None of this blog post should be taken as an endorsement of a heavy-handed enforcement-only strategy to diminish unauthorized immigration. The best way to have well-enforced immigration laws is to have better laws that allow lower skilled immigrants to come permanently or temporarily to work with minimal regulations. Channeling lower skilled workers into the legal market will dramatically reduce the flow of unlawful immigrants, making immigration enforcement along the border more effective—similar to how current border enforcement is more effective during the lousy economy, but without having to suffer low economic growth. Visa overstays are another matter entirely.

A decrease in interior immigration enforcement relative to increased border enforcement does not signal the end of immigration enforcement, as so many are hyperbolically claiming. Interior and border immigration enforcement are substitutes, but border enforcement is much more efficient at actually deterring unauthorized immigration—the actual strategic goal of immigration enforcement.

"*A report from the Urban Institute
also found that children whose
parents were deported or detained
experienced increased rates of crying,
loss of appetite, clingy behavior,
sleeplessness, fear and anxiety.*"

# Deportation Affects the Health and Well Being of Future Generations

*Erika L. Sánchez*

*In the following viewpoint, Erika L. Sánchez examines recent psychological studies that highlight the trauma children experience when one or both of their parents are deported. This manifests not only in emotional disturbances for these children but also in mental health, academic performance, and "overall functioning." If we consider that there are nearly half a million children living in the US with deported parents, the author suggests, we can begin to understand the enormity of the problem. An added issue is that most of these children do not receive the mental health counseling or support that they need in order to succeed. Sánchez is a writer whose work has been published on NBCLatino, in the* Guardian, *on Salon, in* Rolling Stone, *and on Al Jazeera.*

"For Families and Communities, Deportation Means Trauma," by Erika L. Sánchez, Truthout, October 11, 2014. Reprinted by permission.

As you read, consider the following questions:

1. What do studies show about the psychological trauma that children of deported immigrants experience?
2. How does this psychological trauma, according to the experts interviewed in this article, change the trajectory of these children's lives?
3. According to the article, what support do these children need that is not currently being given to them?

Maru Mora-Villalpando lives in fear of deportation. As a community organizer for #Not1More Deportation and an undocumented immigrant from Mexico, her fears are not unfounded. Her nephew was deported in 2008; her cousin was deported in 2010 and she has seen countless other families separated. "I expect that to happen to me as well," she said.

Mora-Villalpando says her 17-year-old daughter constantly worries that she will be deported, particularly because of her activism, which forces her to travel frequently. "We have to be in constant touch. This is how I protect her and lessen her stress that her mother can be taken at any moment," she told Truthout.

Research shows this kind of fear can be profoundly detrimental for children. The study "The Children Left Behind: The Impact of Parental Deportation on Mental Health" notes the crucial role of parent-child relationships in social skills, emotion regulation and self-concept development. Another study, "The Burden of Deportation on Children in Mexican Immigrant Families," based on interviews with 91 parents and 110 children in 80 households, found that the threat of deportation caused fears of separation among children. A report from the Urban Institute also found that children whose parents were deported or detained experienced increased rates of crying, loss of appetite, clingy behavior, sleeplessness, fear and anxiety.

Lisseth Rojas-Flores, Ph.D., an associate professor of marriage and family therapy and licensed psychologist at Fuller Theological

Seminary in Pasadena, California, is currently conducting a study funded by the Foundation for Child Development that assesses the impact of parental detention and deportation on Latino children who are US citizens, and assesses patterns in the use of health and psychological services. The study examines the children's mental health, academic performance and overall functioning. As an immigrant from Colombia, Rojas-Flores is passionate about addressing and researching health disparities in immigrant populations.

"We don't have many studies systematically documenting [the psychological effects of deportations] with standardized measures," Rojas-Flores said. "There is some research documenting that children that are separated from their families are at risk of behavioral problems. We know from research that if a child sees his or her parent arrested, there's a greater negative affect." Some family members, she says, even develop post-traumatic stress syndrome.

Rojas-Flores recounted the story of a family of five she worked with. The three children witnessed the father's arrest and then later visited him at the detention center. As a result of the turmoil, two of the children began developing behavior problems, and the other child began to experience anxiety and became increasingly withdrawn.

Part of the trauma, Rojas-Flores says, is also due to the financial burdens caused by deportations. Because the father was the breadwinner, the family was evicted from their home three times in one year. The mother lost her job because she had to look after her children and advocate for her husband. When he was released from detention six months later, he had lost his job as well.

When her cousin was deported, Mora-Villalpando says that he went from being a provider for his mother to becoming a burden because he was unable to find work in Mexico. She says that the loss of income puts a big strain on families. Most undocumented families depend on each other financially.

She points out that young Latino males are the ones who are most frequently deported, which means they have to leave their partners behind. According to Mora-Villalpando, these women feel guilty all the time because they don't have money to provide for their families. "We don't have access to health care and we [community organizers] don't have the professional skills to deal with that. It's very troublesome to see these families spiral down," she said.

Catherine Wooddell, MSW, a behavioral health therapist, who has conducted individual and family psychotherapy with immigrant women, children, men and families, has seen the emotional damage of deportations firsthand. "There is often a trauma inherent in daily life under the constant threat of deportation," Wooddell told Truthout in an email. "The activities involved in daily living, which the US-born often take for granted, can be profoundly anxiety-provoking for someone who is undocumented or whose family includes undocumented members. Immigrant families are facing constant discriminatory treatment, and for families with members vulnerable to the threat of deportation, each act of discrimination can trigger that fear."

Wooddell says that mixed status families can experience severe anguish if siblings are separated.

"The separation is profoundly painful, and again, they are often unable to understand why they cannot be together," Wooddell said. "This can be seen manifesting as grief with insomnia, nightmares, excessive crying, etc. As they grow older, they come to see the inequity between the conditions under which either sibling lives. This can foster feelings of guilt, similar to 'survivor's guilt,' that can undermine successful coping and school performance."

Sergio Aguilar-Gaxiola, M.D., Ph.D., director of University of California Davis Center for Reducing Health Disparities and professor of Clinical Internal Medicine, agrees that the issue of mental distress among families affected by deportation has been understudied and underreported. "The magnitude of the problem is mind-boggling when we consider there are 2 million parents deported to Mexico leaving behind 400,000 US-born children," he told Truthout. "This is not in the public consciousness in the US.

It's so easy to think about things in such simplistic terms. Putting a face on the issue can change public opinion."

Aguilar-Gaxiola is currently conducting a study with Luis Zayas from the University of Texas in Austin, and Guillermina Natera Rey from the National Institute of Psychiatry (Instituto Nacional de Psiquiatria) of Mexico. Their study, funded by the National Institutes of Health, assesses the distress and psychosocial impact on children with detained or deported parents. They compare the psychological status of three groups: children living in Mexico with deported parents, children in the United States who have been affected by deportation or detention and stayed with other family, and citizen children living with undocumented parents. All the children were ages 8 to 15, right before the severe mental disorders began, he said. According to Aguilar-Gaxiola, this stage in life is characterized by developmental milestones in cognition, behaviors and mental processing.

Aguilar-Gaxiola says that research consistently shows that childhood adversities are the single most powerful predictor of health conditions and early-onset mental illness, such as anxiety, depression and psychological stress. "Children affected directly because parents were deported to Mexico or were detained in the US have significantly high somatic problems," he said. He believes that unless deportations cease, they will continue affecting generations of children.

"What is at stake is the developmental trajectories of these kids," Aguilar-Gaxiola said. "We know that these adversities are also very much related to poverty, neighborhood safety, access to food and lack of facilities to properly exercise." He says families affected by deportations are in desperate need of access to appropriate health care and education.

"The neuropsychological effects of trauma can be passed from one generation to the next, carrying symptoms of anxiety and depression through multiple generations, affecting how and if the next generations will be able to cope with more routine stressors," Wooddell said.

Rojas-Flores says many families don't seek help because of fear and stigma. "Many are afraid for us to go to their homes," she said. "We need to provide a venue and educate them about their rights so they're able to seek the help. A lot of these kids are already at a disadvantage if parents are undocumented. They are often poor and living in poor neighborhoods."

Mora-Villalpando feels the whole community is impacted on every level, which inevitably impacts its future. "There's a constant fear of who's going to be next," she said. "We have met people outside of detention centers who have had two or three family members deported. There's nothing wrong with us. We just happen to lack a piece of paper and we need access to mental health as well."

> *"A secure border is usually demanded
> as a prerequisite of any discussion of
> what to do about the eleven million
> or so unauthorized immigrants
> currently living in the United States;
> but the meaning of a "secure border"
> goes undefined, and the question
> of whether the goal of enforcement
> is preventing all future illegal
> immigration goes unanswered."*

# Zero Illegal Immigration Is Unrealistic

*Theresa Cardinal Brown*

*In the following viewpoint, Theresa Cardinal Brown takes a neutral approach to the otherwise highly politicized immigration debate and concludes that it's impossible to wipe out illegal immigration altogether. However, she suggests, the US government must decide what rate of immigration is acceptable based not only on cost but also on potential ethical considerations. She also suggests that illegal immigration increases with a decrease in viable legal avenues to residence in the United States, and that preventing illegal immigration will cost the US government a substantial amount of money without guaranteeing an absolute return. Brown is director of immigration policy at the Bipartisan Policy Center (BPC).*

"Immigration Enforcement: Is Zero Illegal Immigration Possible?" by Theresa Cardinal Brown, The Board of Trustees of Leland Stanford Junior University, October 26, 2015. Reprinted by permission. Disclaimer: The opinions are the author's own and do not necessarily reflect those of the Bipartisan Policy Center, its funders, or its task force members.

As you read, consider the following questions:

1. According to Brown, is there a historical example of zero illegal immigration? Why or why not?
2. What cost-benefit analysis must the government do, according to Brown, to determine acceptable levels of immigration?
3. What other considerations must the US government reflect on in regard to immigration policy?

A s the 2016 presidential campaign kicks into high gear, voters are hearing calls from many candidates to step up immigration enforcement and secure the border. Such calls are not new, and the suggested methods for doing so—border walls, employment verification, and even increased deportations—have been part of the debate over immigration for decades. Most of these calls for action, however, are short on metrics. A secure border is usually demanded as a prerequisite of any discussion of what to do about the eleven million or so unauthorized immigrants currently living in the United States; but the meaning of a "secure border" goes undefined, and the question of whether the goal of enforcement is preventing all future illegal immigration goes unanswered.

The Bipartisan Policy Center recently published a report on enforcement metrics, noting that the government has never consistently published metrics on the success of its current enforcement efforts against unauthorized migration. The report suggests a specific set of metrics that would allow all sides in the immigration debate to be on the same page regarding the current state of border security and interior enforcement.

That report, however, does not call for a specific goal of zero illegal immigration. In fact, the report notes that there has never been anywhere a fully secure border. Even East Germany, at the height of the Cold War, with thirty-thousand soldiers, shoot-to-kill orders, and perpetual surveillance of the population by secret police, could only prevent 95 percent of the attempts to get to West Germany. Although I do not have empirical evidence, I think one would be hard-pressed to find any border, enforcement, or regulatory system of any kind created by any government that has been 100 percent successful in preventing or deterring unlawful activity.

So if getting to zero illegal immigration is unrealistic, what level of enforcement is realistic?

Basic economics would postulate that a certain "natural" level of immigration would be expected at a given level of enforcement activity. Enforcement agencies (and policy makers) would need to determine whether that level is acceptable and whether the marginal cost of attempting to reduce the level is worth it. To make such judgments, however, one needs to know how much enforcement effect the current level of spending and resources has achieved. So we are back to metrics.

Assuming that we did have the metrics with which to make such decisions, and assuming that some unlawful migration will not be prevented, deterred, or detected by enforcement, how should the government determine where to focus its enforcement resources? This is the foundation for a discussion of "prosecutorial discretion," meaning is any specific unlawful activity of sufficient severity to be worth the cost to the government to go after it? As a broad policy measure, this requires setting priorities on which are the most important activities to prevent or deter. In general, the government tends to place threats to life, property, and national security at the top of that list.

Also to be considered is enforcement that protects the integrity of the system, that is, enforcement aimed at having a deterrent effect on the overall level of unlawful activity. When it comes to immigration, however, determining what enforcement activities can successfully deter unauthorized migration is tricky.

As our metrics paper explains, migration flows are based on various incentives and the cost-benefit determinations of millions of individuals across the globe. Whether the enforcement efforts of a government to prevent such migration factor into those determinations is also individualized. The incentives for immigration, lawful or unlawful, vary by individual but have historically included such factors as economic opportunity, family reunification, and improved safety and security. In other words, home country conditions and expectations for improvement in those conditions are a large factor, as are the chances of improving those conditions by migrating to the receiving country. The costs of migration are weighed against those incentives. The costs in this case include both the actual monetary costs of making the migration journey (transportation costs, document costs, facilitator costs) and the potential risks to the individual along the way. The chance of successfully entering the new country is also a part of the equation.

The choice between lawful or unlawful migration is also part of the decision. The factors in this choice include the chances of obtaining a legal visa (meeting requirements and qualifications, cost to apply, length of the process) versus the dangers and costs of unlawful migration and the chances of successfully crossing the border. In general, those who are able to migrate lawfully would normally choose that route. Those who are unable to do so because they cannot qualify under the legal migration scheme or cannot afford the costs may consider unlawfully migrating if the other incentives are high enough.

Note that the chances of apprehension are only one of the many factors involved in the migration decision. In our paper, we note that the deterrent effect of apprehension is not linear. In other words, to the migrant, the chance of apprehension has to be high (well more than 80 percent) before the number of attempts necessary for success is higher than a handful. Thus the costs to the government of achieving higher rates of apprehension are likely to be much higher than the costs to the migrant of additional attempts, meaning the cost of achieving more deterrence, especially in the face of strong factors, is likely to be high.

This means policy makers need to look at options to affect other parts of the migration decision. Employment verification would reduce the likelihood of getting unlawful employment. The availability of jobs outside the legal labor market, however, would mitigate that impact, requiring additional resources to ensure the enforcement of the employment verification regime. Additional interior enforcement to decrease the likelihood of establishing residence could also affect the migration decision, but with more than eleven million unauthorized currently resident, the costs of such enforcement would be in the billions of dollars.

Setting aside the moral and macroeconomic considerations of such high levels of enforcement, with sufficient incentives, a certain number of individuals will attempt to enter the United States unlawfully, and some portion of those will succeed. Policy makers must determine how many dollars they want to allocate to immigration enforcement versus other government priorities given that we can, in reality, never get to zero illegal immigration.

# Periodical and Internet Sources Bibliography

*The following articles have been selected to supplement the diverse views presented in this chapter.*

Illona Bray, "Legal Reasons a U.S. Immigrant May Be Deported," AllLaw. http://www.alllaw.com/articles/nolo/us-immigration/legal-reasons -immigrant-may-be-deported.html.

Damien Cave, "Long Border, Endless Struggle," *New York Times*, March 2, 2013. http://www.nytimes.com/2013/03/03/world/americas/border -security-hard-to-achieve-and-harder-to-measure.html.

Jacqueline Charles, "U.S. Government Quietly Resumes Deportations to Haiti," *Miami Herald*, November 8, 2016. http://www.miamiherald .com/news/nation-world/world/americas/haiti/article113396383.html.

*The Economist*, "Secure Enough: Spending Billions More on Fences and Drones Will Do More Harm Than Good," June 22, 2013. http://www .economist.com/news/united-states/21579828-spending-billions-more -fences-and-drones-will-do-more-harm-good-secure-enough.

Joshua Gillin, "Terrorists from Groups Besides ISIS Crossing U.S.-Mexico Border, U.S. Rep. Ron DeSantis Says," Politifact, April 4, 2016. http:// www.politifact.com/florida/statements/2016/apr/04/ron-desantis /terrorists-groups-besides-isis-crossing-us-mexico-.

Ana Gomez, "How Trump Can Ramp up Deportations," *USA Today*, November 18, 2016. http://www.usatoday.com/story/news /nation/2016/11/18/president-elect-donald-trump-deportation -increase-undocumented-immigrants/94022680.

Ana Gonzalez-Barrera and Jens Manuel Krogstad, "U.S. Immigrant Deportations Declined in 2014, But Remain Near Record High," Pew Research, August 31, 2016. http://www.pewresearch.org/fact -tank/2016/08/31/u-s-immigrant-deportations-declined-in-2014-but -remain-near-record-high.

Garrett M. Graff, "The Green Monster: How the Border Patrol Became America's Most Out-of-Control Law Enforcement Agency," Politico, November/December 2014. http://www.politico.com/magazine /story/2014/10/border-patrol-the-green-monster-112220.

Anna O. Law, "Lie, Damned Lies, and Obama's Deportation Statistics," *Washington Post*, April 21, 2014. https://www.washingtonpost.com /news/monkey-cage/wp/2014/04/21/lies-damned-lies-and-obamas -deportation-statistics/?utm_term=.30cb67d3fcd2.

Miriam Valverde, "Trump Right on Obama's Deportation Numbers, Wrong About Nobody Talking About It," *Politifact*, October 21, 2016. http:// www.politifact.com/truth-o-meter/statements/2016/oct/21/donald -trump/trump-right-deportation-numbers-wrong-talks-about-.

# For Further Discussion

## Chapter 1

1. What groups of people might be particularly vulnerable under the US immigration system? Why?
2. What are some ways in which women might have more difficulty immigrating (legally or illegally) to the United States?
3. Do you think the rich should have more opportunities to legally immigrate to the United States and other countries than the poor and middle class? Why or why not?

## Chapter 2

1. In your opinion, would Muslim immigrants from war-torn nations like Syria pose more of a security threat than other immigrants? Why or why not?
2. What vetting system is in place for immigrants entering the United States? Do you think it needs to be reformed in any way?
3. Do you think that security and humanitarian concerns can be reconciled in practice in regard to US immigration? Why or why not?

## Chapter 3

1. What do you think about the data presented in this chapter? Do you think there is enough information presented to reach a conclusion about whether or not illegal immigrants hurt the US economy?
2. Why might undocumented workers be less likely to use government services than legal immigrants or citizens?

3. Do you think the economy would be harmed if large amounts of undocumented workers were deported from the United States? Why or why not?

## Chapter 4

1. What do you think about border control and interior deportations? Do you think they work as complements or as substitutes? Which system, in your opinion, seems to be more effective?
2. Why do you think the southern US border is more tightly controlled than the northern US border?
3. Have you ever—or has anyone you've known—ever experienced deportation? How did it affect them? How do you think it would affect families?

# Organizations to Contact

*The editors have compiled the following list of organizations concerned with the issues debated in this book. The descriptions are derived from materials provided by the organizations. All have publications or information available for interested readers. The list was compiled on the date of publication of the present volume; the information provided here may change. Be aware that many organizations take several weeks or longer to respond to inquiries, so allow as much time as possible.*

**American Immigration Lawyers Association (AILA)**
1331 G Street NW, Suite 300
Washington, DC 20005
(202) 507-7600
email: advocacy@aila.org
website: http://www.aila.org

AILA is an organization comprised of over seven thousand immigration lawyers and law professors. Its website includes contact information for lawyers specializing in immigration law, as well as access to their monthly journal, *AILA's Immigration Law Today.*

**Farmworker Justice**
1126 16th Street NW, Suite 270
Washington, DC 20036
(202) 293-5420
contact: http://www.farmworkerjustice.org/contact
website: http://www.farmworkerjustice.org

Farmworker Justice is a nonprofit organization dedicated to helping and empowering seasonal farmworkers and migrants through providing educational programs, advocacy, and other forms of support.

**Immigrant Legal Resource Center (ILRC)**
1663 Mission Street, Suite 602
San Francisco, CA 94103
(415) 255-9499
email: pgarcia@ilrc.org
website: https://www.ilrc.org

The ILRC provides legal training, educational materials, and advocacy to immigrants in the interest of securing their rights in the United States.

**Lutheran Immigration and Refugee Service (LIRS)**
700 Light Street
Baltimore, MD 21230
(410) 230-2700
email: lirs@lirs.org
website: http://lirs.org

Founded in 1939, LIRS has welcomed more than 500,000 refugees and immigrants and worked to secure their rights. Those interested can volunteer, donate, or foster refugee children.

**Mexican American Legal Defense and Education Fund (MALDEF)**
634 South Spring Street, 11th Floor
Los Angeles, CA 90014
(213) 629-2512
contact: http://www.maldef.org/contact/index.html
website: http://www.maldef.org

A leading Latino litigation, advocacy, and educational organization, MALDEF was founded in 1968 and continues to work to foster policy that protects the civil rights of Mexican Americans.

### National Asian Pacific American Legal Consortium (NAPALC)
1140 Connecticut Avenue NW, Suite 1200
Washington, DC 20036
(202) 296-2300
contact: http://advancingjustice-aajc.org/contact-us
website: http://advancingjustice-aajc.org

Founded in 1991, this organization works to secure the legal and civil rights of Asian Pacific Americans through litigation, public education, and public policy.

### National Council of La Raza (NCLR)
1111 19th Street NW, Suite 1000
Washington, DC 20036
(202) 785-1670
email: info@nclr.org
website: http://www.nclr.org

One of the largest Latino rights organizations in the world, the NCLR works on policy analysis and advocacy for Latinos in the United States on the national level.

### National Immigration Forum (NIF)
220 I Street NE, Suite 220
Washington, DC 20002
(202) 544-0004
contact: http://immigrationforum.org/contact
website: http://immigrationforum.org

The NIF works to provide information to policy makers, the media, and the public about the importance of multiculturalism and immigration in the United States. It publishes a variety of journals, including the *Immigration Policy Handbook*.

**The National Network for Immigrant and Refugee Rights (NNIRR)**
310 8th Street, Suite 307
Oakland, CA 94607
(510) 465-1984
email: nnirrinfo@nnirr.org
website: http://www.nnirr.org/drupal

This coalition of over two hundred immigrant rights groups promotes the rights of all immigrants and refugees, no matter their immigration status.

**Office of Migration and Refugee Services**
United States Conference of Catholic Bishops
3211 4th Street NE
Washington, DC 20017
(202) 541-3000
website: http://www.usccb.org/about/migration-and-refugee-services

As part of the United States Conference of Catholic Bishops, this organization works to implement pro-immigration policy for the Catholic Church.

# Bibliography of Books

Tyler Anbinder, *City of Dreams: The 400-Year Epic History of Immigrant New York*. Boston, MA: Houghton Mifflin Harcourt, 2016.

Stephan Bauman and Matthew Soerens, *Seeking Refuge: On the Shores of the Global Refugee Crisis*. Chicago, IL: Moody Publishers, 2016.

Dale Hanson Bourke, *Immigration: Tough Questions, Direct Answers* (The Skeptic's Guide). Downers Grove, IL: IVP Books, 2014.

Ilona Bray, *U.S. Immigration Made Easy*. Berkeley, CA: NOLO, 2015.

Aviva Chomsky, *Undocumented: How Immigration Became Illegal*. New York, NY: Beacon Press, 2014.

Roger Daniels, *Guarding the Golden Door: American Immigration Policy and Immigrants Since 1882*. New York, NY: Hill and Wang, 2005.

Edwidge Danticat, *Mama's Nightingale: A Story of Immigration and Separation*. New York, NY: Dial Books, 2015.

David A. Gerber, *American Immigration: A Very Short Introduction*. New York, NY: Oxford University Press, 2011.

Tom Gjelten, *A Nation of Nations: A Great American Immigration Story*. New York, NY: Simon & Schuster, 2016.

Reece Jones, *Violent Borders: Refugees and the Right to Move*. New York, NY: Verso Books, 2016.

Patrick Kingsley, *The New Odyssey: The Story of the Twenty-First Century Refugee Crisis*. New York, NY: Liveright, 2011.

Thanhha Lai, *Inside Out and Back Again*. New York, NY: HarperCollins, 2013.

Linda Sue Park, *A Long Walk to Water: Based on a True Story*. Boston, MA: HMH Books for Young Readers, 2011.

Ben Rawlence, *City of Thorns: Nine Lives in the World's Largest Refugee Camp*. New York, NY: Picador, 2017.

Margriet Ruurs and Falah Raheem, *Stepping Stones: A Refugee Family's Journey*. Victoria, CA: Orca Book Publishers, 2016.

Bruce Thatcher, *Immigration: How to Avoid Its Perils and Make It Work*. CreateSpace, 2012.

Luis Alberto Urrea, *The Devil's Highway: A True Story*. New York, NY: Back Bay Books, 2005.

Marina Villa, *Leaving Castro's Cuba: The Story of an Immigrant Family*. CreateSpace, 2012.

Isabel Wilkerson, *The Warmth of Other Suns: The Epic Story of America's Great Migration*. New York, NY: Vintage, 2011.

Tom K. Wong, *The Politics of Immigration: Partisanship, Demographic Change, and American National Identity*. New York, NY: Oxford University Press, 2017.

# Index